Cyber Danger

GCC Countries & Qatar

Cyber Danger

Computing Danger

GCC & Developing Countries

Road Map for Cyber Security for Qatar and GCC Countries

Dr. Mohammed Al-Dorani

Dedications

I would like to dedicate this book to my wonderful wife Gloria, for without her love and support throughout the many years of our marriage, my life would not be as beautiful. Also, it is my beloved daughters Leila and Sarah, who are the source of my motivation, as I continue my life in pursuing the highest levels of personal abilities.

About the Author

Dr. Mohammed Al-Dorani was born in the year 1954 in the geographical area of Doha, Qatar. At the time of his earliest years, Qatar was a nation that few knew of. But as the ability of the extraction techniques and knowhow of developing the areas international oil and gas sector, were able to be accessed through those certain nations, the gulf nations were given an opportunity. And in that time frame, there was given to the population of the gulf region an appreciation to uplift itself, through their connection to those regions of certain other ability.

Dr. Mohammed Al-Dorani came from a strong family, whose history of that of his father and mother were of that history of the 30's of the Gulf area of Arabia. As the young Mohammed knew that his strongest desire, was to achieve the highest level possible in terms of his education. He, through his strong will and determination, achieved his Masters degree, as well as his Ph.D degree by the age of thirty.

Dr. Mohammed Al-Dorani graduated from the George Washington Graduate School of Business with special emphasis in technology. The subject of his doctorate thesis was on developing a central information system data base for the Six Gulf Countries.

After Dr. Mohammed Al-Dorani attained his Ph.D., he was appointed by his government of Qatar, to represent that nation at the Gulf Cooperation Council located in Riyadh, Saudi Arabia.

Dr. Mohammed Al-Dorani served as "The Director of Post, Telegraph, and Telecommunication" for the Six Gulf Nations, remaining in his work there for eight years. While having a full time job at the GCC, he taught senior level courses at the Computer Science College at King Saud University in Riyadh, in addition he consulted for Sabic and Al-yamama publishing on computing and networking systems. Dr. Mohammed is married to his American wife, Mrs. Gloria Karen Byers Al-Dorani and has two daughters, Leila and Sarah.

After serving his government through Qatar's Ministry of Finance and serving at the Gulf Cooperation Council, he left Qatar and became the Acting CEO for the Iridium project of the Middle East sector. The project was a multi-billion dollar global effort, that was centered through the Motorola company and involved the participation of over one hundred. Dr. Al-Dorani also managed as a General Manager and for 10 years Abdulla Abdulghani & Bro, company, one of the largest family-owned business that own the sole distribution of Toyota and Lexus vehicles in the State of Qatar.

Dr. Mohammed Al-Dorani is currently managing his private international company, and works with his wife Gloria, and his daughters in Asian regions such as China, as well as the Middle East through his business efforts.

Contents

Introduction: i

Chapter One: GCC countries & Qatar 1

Chapter Two: Nations Cyber Attacks, Worms & Viruses Used 8

Iranian Nuclear Facility & Stuxnet...**11**

Georgia and Estonia & DDoS...**18**

Israel attack on Syrian nuclear reactor...**20**

Middle East: Flame, Dugu & DDoS..**21**

Dugu **21**

Flame...**23**

DDoS..**27**

Shutting Down the Water System in USA:..**28**

The Syrian Electronic Army (SEA):...**32**

Chapter Three: Corporate Cyber Attacks **35**

International Monetary Fund (IMF)..**35**

Sony:...**37**

Chapter Four: Hacking Threats..**50**

Constant Threats..**52**

No Fear:...**55**

Three levels of hacking:..**56**

Why do they Hack and How?...**60**

Types of Viruses, and Worms used:..**66**

Chapter Five: Corporate Vulnerability..**69**

US Government & Technology Companies...70

Corporate Valuable Assests Protection: Information & Money 72

Prevent & Restore...74

a) The Corporate Token...75

b) Firewalls, and Intrusion-detection systems.....................................77

c) Anti-virus Programs...80

d) Back UP Systems...81

e) Cyber Security Auditing:...83

Chapter Six: Role of CIOs/IT Managers & Cyber Security Experts.......87

Budget Issues & Cyber Strategy...90

Security Deployment Measures & Cyber Attack Testing 93

Cost & Hacking Insurance Policy..95

Wired Countries & Hacking:...98

Chapter Seven: Nations and National Cyber Security........................103

a) Cyber War...103

b) Cyber Crime..103

c) Cyber Espionage 103

Recent Spy Cases:...104

Kenya:..104

Iran:...108

Developing countries & Mobility Threats...110

Chapter Eight: Softare Companies: Oracle & SAP............................121

Oracle & SAP Cyber Security Approach..124

Oracle and SAP Bills of Materials...132

Chapter Nine: GCC and Cyber Security...141

GCC Countries & Qatar Cyber Approach..151

National Cyber Security Strategy & Qatar......................................160

Chapter Ten: GCC Nations Protection against Cyber Threats............................172

Defense Strategy..179

Small Nation cyber defense: Qatar **181**

Chapter Eleven: The New Cyber Command Center: Military Approach............**193**

The Chinese Model:...**196**

Chapter Twelve: Road Map: The New Cyber Command Center........................**213**

Intelligence/Military Cyber Security Command......................................**214**

a) Staffing Requirements...**220**

b) Motivational Issues...**224**

c) Educational Matters...**225**

Set up of The New Cyber...**227**

One major hurdle **232**

Country-Wide Cyber Security Audit & Upgrade.....................................**235**

Chapter Thirteen: GCC Nations: Cyber Command Centers:

   Final Thoughts **238**

Glossary..**246**

References..**253**

Index...**264**

Introduction
Cyber Danger & GCC Countries

Since I was student in my during my college times and right after I was accepted to Graduate School, I have had a keen interest in Information Systems. This was even before the coming age of the Internet, which revolutionized the entire world. When I was a student in graduate school, we used the first generation of personal computers, which were connected on-line, through the smallest bandwidth to the mainframe computer of the university. The word processors on the personal computers were so simple that you would be able to write small numbers of pages, before your memory size was full and therefore it was impossible to write a document consisting of hundreds of pages. So, our only salvation was to use the word processor and writing tools on our university's computer mainframe. It was revolutionary for us to be able to write our dissertations and research papers at home and have them printed out on the computer campus. Our fear at that time was that our hard work in printed papers, might be either misplaced or stolen. We definitely knew that if such act would take place, it would have been an inside job within the administration room of the Computer Center. There were chances of giving our printed papers to someone else by accident, but then this could not be easily done as there was a name and print job number on each paper printed.

Today, most work is done on laptops, which contain a huge memory size and storage capabilities that almost rival the sizes of larger computers that were used back during my graduate studies in the 80's. These small portable devices allowed us to write multiple books without any sight of technological troubles. We could print our work from these devices with the full privacy being either at home or in the office. We could also send work across the vast space of the internet to any publisher or person without worrying about the limitations of bandwidth transmission. However, the issue of concern to many is how secure is your work when you send it out, or even when you open your laptop. The possibility, is that your hard work stored and transmitted on your lap top might be stolen without even knowing it. The Fear of losing everything by professional hackers and government agencies that might be spying on you, knowing your every stroke you type and copying and spoofing everything on your devices to collect and store has become the now nightmare scenario not only on the individual front, but also on company and national fronts.

When the internet was created as a basic idea in the 1960s, the defense department funded the project through DARPA (Defense Department's Advanced Research Project Agency) mainly to be used for research and development in connecting major US universities including MIT, Stanford, and others. The project was called ARPANET (Advance Research Project Agency Network). The history of the internet is well documented for those who would like to read more about it. The Internet has done good things for human beings, with this human development, especially increasing the power of information sharing and access. With this freedom of information exchange and sharing, comes many vulnerabilities with it. Hackers and ill-intended individuals or nations have used the internet in such a powerful way as to launch attacks using viruses and worms, also planting trapdoors and logic bombs for future hacking and cyber attacks. The internet has been open for people to exchange emails and share different types of information, and of course to access a vast pool of knowledge which is spread across the globe. Millions of people use the internet on a daily basis, and this powerful medium has became indispensable to many.

The evolution of telephony from the basic calling medium to powerful hand held mobile devices that not only connects you to the Internet from any place and anywhere, it also lets you use the mobile device as an actual mobile computer, where you can do almost anything you want sitting at home, at work, or being mobile on the road. These mobile devices have become the actual computers and they are getting smarter and filled with more new technological features. People now use their Ipad, mobile phones, small laptops and many upcoming mobile devices, more than using desk top computers. This does not mean that desk top computers will disappear soon. No, it is still a valuable tool in the office environment and in many homes, where they offer greater capabilities and utilities in terms of storage and memory capabilities, more than mobile devices. We will witness similar advancement in the mobile devices by them having a higher storage and memory capability. Small mobile phones can have the power of a desk top computer of a 5 years ago. At this rate, the dependency on the mobility will be stronger, and therefore connectivity to the internet and computer networks using wifi (wireless access using mobile devices including phones, ipads, and desk top computers to local the computer or server of the intended premises to be connected to. The vast numbers of mobile devices and other computer systems accessing the internet at a huge rate, has opened doors to hackers and hacktivists of either criminal groups, individuals, or nations to launch on a daily basis cyber attacks through the worldwide internet. The rate of attacks using viruses, malwares, and other types of hacking techniques is so staggering, that security companies are creating anti viruses that cannot and will not keep up with their fixes and updated software to clean up the infected computers and network systems. There are unfortunately thousands of computers that are infected, and many companies and individuals do not know about them as they stay stealth. Security software companies who produce commercial private anti-viruses and intrusion-detection programs cannot keep up with these new viruses and worms produced by hackers. However, they can help in cleaning them and providing tools and the ability to find them. Powerful nations, that many security companies belong to, are not fully sharing their technologies with the nations they are selling to. This is because they are under pressure by the spy agencies of their nations to maintain superiority in terms of their governmental ability to hack into the country's computers.

Some nations have come up with regulations to stop intelligence agencies from spying on their own citizens locally and internationally. However, this practice is going on at full speed. Hardware, software, and network communication systems are real targets, and no anti-virus program can stop them. They are given the belief that these companies when they carry out the sale of these computing and networking systems, and provided with the necessary training, installation, and implementation and service maintenance, that their computer networks and various devices are secure, and many assurances are constantly given to decision makers within the country that is all well, and the country's networking and computing environment is virus free due to implemented anti-viruses programs. Unfortunately, many nations, and in particular the GCC six countries, do not realize the fact that in many of their governmental agencies and companies, their computer systems have been infected and the anti-viruses used and sold to them by international security commercial companies cannot successfully remove many different viruses and worms launched by the hackers. With any attempt to clean up these computers, hackers always have their way in coming up with new versions of viruses and worms. Difficulties for these GCC developing nations are the technological in-capabilities to understand that work of viruses and worms. Lethal viruses that are launched by advanced nations and hacking groups, are not the types of viruses and worms that are easily discovered by these anti-virus programs. They can be stay stealth in the computers' backdoor style and await instructions to launch an attack or to evade any detection. These trapdoors are the hardest to find and currently existing security companies with their anti viruses, are not capable of finding them, and if they do, they do not have the capability to remove them. These logic bombs are probably now in every major installation, especially major infrastructures such as oil and gas companies, electrical power grid systems, and various other critical infrastructures that the economy of the six GCC countries depend on them in their daily life. These countries have to setup their priorities the right way when it comes to cyber threats and attacks. They have to be aware of the danger which currently exists and is coming in near future. This is a matter of national security to these developing nations. We will discuss this in more detail through the book with various examples of cyber attacks and hackers doing so much damage on other nations including some of the countries in the GCC countries and the Middle East.

Cyber Security therefore has been in my mind and became my most interesting subject since graduating from Graduate School. I first I learned about NSA and spying when I read my first book on the subject called "The White Palace", during 1980's, when not many people had heard of this agency outside the Washington DC beltway. The agency is vast with powerful technologies and financial funding. It has farms outside the capital with hundreds of super power computers connected to multiple powerful artificial intelligence tools, and applications that can decipher any language and decompose any message into its' basic. It has multiple sites across the globe with satellites that can sweep all electronic calls and messages using the most sophisticated low orbiting satellites relaying emails, signals, messages, etc., to these super computers for collection, analysis, and disseminations to various analysts and experts. The budget of this agency exceeds all other agencies within the US government.

Computers and information systems are my favorite subject which motivated me to specialize in this field, during my doctorate program. Being from Qatar i was one of the few Gulf citizens to go to America and attain my doctorate degree, graduating at the young age of 30. This was a major accomplishment personally for me and my family. Living in Washington D.C., the capital of the United States of America, gave me, like many foreign students, the motivation to get into the worldly subject by the nature of being in the political city center of America. The capital having the Congress and major Governmental Agencies and International establishments, not to mention the major libraries and museums, which are a great source of information. My interest was in Information Systems, Telecommunication and Cyber Technology which was in those years in its' infancy in terms of commercial use. The Cyber technology was more advanced than we thought. In those years, in the 80's, the coverage and even the mentioning of cyber systems, spying, cyber wars, cyber espionage, and other related internet attacks or cyber attacks, were the subject of many Hollywood movies. You would never hear of these topics or subjects in print media or newspapers, let alone on TV programs. The mentioning of the name of the NSA was so anonymous that not many people even in D.C. had heard of such a name. People like me, who were intrigued by the subject, would of course dig deeper and discover that the world of cyber attacks and espionage are not as new as we hear about nowadays in the media and with so many cases reported which I will mention about in this book, about how such brazen attacks are not only enacted on individuals, but also on corporations, and finally on nations. These attacks can destroy not only files, and steal your passwords and messages, they can hack into your phone calls and emails. It can also disrupt the nations' infrastructure, either through telecommunication systems, banks, and other major infrastructures, so that many countries are rendered defenseless. Many nations have lost wars due to these cyber attacks by other nations not realizing that advanced countries in such technologies can make less developed country defense systems useless and defenseless because their radars, advanced defense systems, or computer operating rooms, and industrial control centers, have been attacked by sophisticated viruses, worms, and Trojan horses, amongst many types of cyber attacks either sent over the internet or entered into the computing operating system of a corporation or a government institution by an inside job.

In writing this book, I would like to focus on the subject of cyber security and its' impact on small nations that have the great ambition to be big in terms of achieving dreams. However, at the same time these developing nations are vulnerable to cyber attacks, that can devastate and cripple their economies, and infrastructures. In this book which will be part one of several writings to come in near future, I would like to focus on the six Gulf GCC countries and use Qatar as an example to other neighboring countries. Qatar is a member of the six gulf nations including Saudi Arabia, Kuwait, Oman, Bahrain, and the UAE. They belong to the Gulf Cooperation Council. The concept of this council was based after the European Union. My doctorate dissertation was on the Gulf Cooperation Council, focusing on building its' computer and network infrastructures. Immediately following the completion of my doctorate program, I was appointed as the first one of my country in that generation, to serve at the organization of the Gulf Cooperation Council in Riyadh, Saudi Arabia, where its headquarters is based, and is the capital of the Kingdom of Saudi Arabia. I was assigned to be the Director of the Post, Computers and Telecommunications departments for the six Gulf Nations. Therefore, in focusing on the GCC Countries, I am discussing the six countries as they share similar strategies and plans with regards to Cyber Security. They work together through the Information Systems and Telecommunications committees, which I chaired during my work for eight years at this organization. My understanding of the working environment of theses six nations, allows me to translate such work of one nation into the other five member countries, regardless of geographical and population scale of each country, but with emphasis on similarity with regards to cyber security and plans to develop the cyber command and control centers for the Gulf Cooperation Council and each GCC country.

Chapter One

GCC countries

These small size nations namely Saudi Arabia, Kuwait, Qatar, the United Arab Emirates, Oman and Bahrain are considered the wealthiest in the world with a per capita income which exceeds 60,000-90,000 US dollars. The total population of the six countries does not exceed 60 million. Local population is less than 25 million, and the remaining are foreigners working for a living in a strange land. The economies of these six Gulf nations are very much dependent on the Oil and Gas sector. Therefore, 90 percent of their income and wealth comes from the sale of oil and gas to other nations. They however are not equal in terms of oil and gas wealth. For example, Saudi Arabia given its' vast size has the highest wealth coming in from the sale of oil. The six countries decided with the coming of this wealth to embrace and meet the demands of its' population and government entities, and with the help of Western companies in the importing and installing as many of commercial and technological available products. The proliferation of the applications and the implementation of computing, networking, communications, and the internet have become so prevalent in government and private entities across these countries' daily life which has become totally dependent on them.

The GCC countries have accomplished so much in a very short period of time with their leaders who are committed to their visions, and plans, or financial power to achieve the goals visualized in the countries' 20-30 years vision. Qatar for example, has entered the news globally when this small nation with no chance of winning a major sporting event, was able to achieve the impossible, to win the hosting of the World Cup, soccer's biggest event in the world, where over 2 billion people view these matches. Recently, the country has become a capital of major world major sporting champions. Not only in sport but also in conferences and major international events. Qatar like its' sister GCC countries spearheads worldwide investments buying major international properties and companies. Major world-class acquisitions and investments have taken place abroad. The GCC countries have been transformed completely within a time span of ten years making them the most progressive developing nation amongst the developing world. When a visitor comes back to these countries after an absence of many years, they do not recognize it. In fact, he or she would be astonished to see such dramatic change and progress. This progress has not stopped. These countries are expanding not only in their infrastructure but also in their population with many people, especially workers who are building huge infrastructures to cater to the biggest sporting and business events in the world. Meanwhile to stay safe from the dangers that would hamper such developments, these countries have been on a massive political quest to make friends, not only regionally but also internationally. This of course causes many nations to envy these small countries and many nations to even consider them as so aggressive that they have acted against them especially in cyber space, where various attacks took place using the internet and other Telecommunications means, thereby disrupting many sites and closing businesses especially in banking, education, and the oil and gas sector.

Given all the above, the subject of cyber security, and protecting the GCC nations infrastructures, is the subject of this book. As read so many articles in the news media about hackings sites and stealing passwords, identification numbers, or email addresses, there are vast types of hacking that are extremely damaging to nations' infrastructures and this is not done only in using the internet, which we will shed light on this book, but also on insiders within the nations' establishments, that have a certain agenda to damage the nations' infrastructures.

The awareness of the cyber advanced nations such as the United States, China, Russia, and as many as 20 to 30 nations that have had their various computer and communications systems compromised and hacked by other nations or groups of hacktivists most likely working with other nations. Only now, I been able to realize this in the past five to ten years, as to the National Interests and potential damage they can bring to nations' infrastructures.

The GCC countries are committed to the advancement of the internet, computing, and communication networking. They set up a government gateway to interconnect their e-government systems to enable each country and its' population to access to other country's networks, navigate and do business. This way they can enable the level of availability of each other e-government websites with ministries working closely with the public sectors providing fast Internet Services. What is reported in these meetings, is that Internet connections amongst the six countries will be through a gateway, a "GCC-Gateway". The security agenda and mainly cyber attacks and threats that possibly would come from such interconnection has become of the topic of various agendas of the GCC's higher ministerial committees. For good work in creating such a gateway, there is also the side effect of the adaptation of internet connectivity and computing technology within these countries. Hackers ability to launch cyber attacks have widened now. We hope such gateways will have the necessary firewalls, intrusion-detection programs, and anti-viruses to mitigate any cyber threats and potential hacking risks, but not necessarily stop, as hackers will always have the technology to be on the offensive regardless what defensive means the six countries put in place. I still would like to see better organization when it comes to cyber security regarding the GCC countries if they are serious in protecting their vital interests and infrastructures. This might be a difficult job to undertake given that administrative bureaucratic side of government officials in charge of internet security. They are so busy and overwhelmed with the daily issues of hacking coming in country that they are not even comprehending how to coordinate with each other and provide unified policy and coordinated strategies. We will discuss such bureaucratic weaknesses, and I will illustrate how government administrative officials cannot fulfill necessary cyber security requirements. Therefore, we will recommend an approach that has a more Military side to it, as it has happened with the European Union when they decided to hand over cyber security matters to Nato. It is Nato's Cyber Command and Control Center which was born for the protection of the Euro members countries territories from which there are cyber attacks. Will the GCC Council do the same? In my doctorate dissertation I have written about the interconnection of the six GCC countries in terms of communication networking, and setting up different data bases within the governments' entities to be interconnected with GCC's centralized data repository. At the time of writing of my dissertation, threats of cyber attacks, and the manifestation of wide spread worms and viruses were almost rare to hear or read about. If they were available they were mostly in more advanced countries' hands, such as the USA and some European countries. Russia and China were not as advanced in cyber threats during 1980's, and therefore threats would come from nations attacking other nations, and not as its' proliferated across the globe where no one can acquire worms and viruses in the black market and do not require technical skills to launch a cyber attacks. This would make the job for securing infrastructures and gateways of the six GCC countries even more difficult. The military approach to cyber security would be one preferred option for these GCC countries. A preferred cyber command and control model and road map of how to implement it will be discussed in later chapters in more detail.

China realized that in order to be independent from foreign control not only in terms of using different computer and communication technologies, also it did not want to be out of use and adaptation of such wonderful technologies that would help its economy. However, it needed a new strategy that would combine both cyber and information protection and at the same time have Internet and Information technologies available to those populations and businesses. China can and has been able to deter itself from many other nations hacking and spying on it, by using its own technological developments, and also closing loopholes by not allowing certain western technologies to be utilized within country and in its' various government as well as private companies. As an example, Microsoft Windows had a total monopoly on the operating systems of all personal computers, until Apple came out with its' Macintosh operating system. China did not accept Windows operating system which is well known and has major security flaws, and which be hacked by hacktivists and intelligence agencies from Western countries. China never trusted the West and in particular Microsoft Windows, and therefore it forced Microsoft to allow China access to end its' monopolistic source code of the Windows Operating System by handing it over to Chinese regulators. Similar situations have taken place with other companies such as IBM and HP for example. The Linux operating system, which is actually an open source code can be accessed easily and modified. China did not trust this open source code and therefore created its' own Linux and named it Red Flag. The same goes for hardware systems, and routers. This shows how cautious the Chinese are when it comes to Western technologies operating within its' borders. China created major telecommunications and computer companies with huge investment in human resources, to develop its' own hardware routers, and programs similar to the West. Now Huawei is as big as Cisco, and is not only selling its' network routers in China but around the world.

Lack of trust by China with Western Technology is understandable, and many nations should use an approach similar to China. The GCC countries are so dependent on Western technologies, that it has become an open field for hacking and spying, and potential cyber attacks that might one day not only cripple a certain industry or infrastructure, but it could bring the economy to stand still. We will discuss the Chinese model when it comes to utilizing and implementing information and communication systems within its' borders. We will see if this Chinese model can fit the GCC countries, not necessarily as a total package but in its' partiality.

Chapter Two
Nations Cyber Attacks
Worms and Viruses Used

Many nations are now at war with one another. We are not talking about use of conventional wars such as troops, bombs, and other heavy artilleries with foot soldiers, or bombing from the skies, but cyber wars. Nations recruited many spies and utilized all means of intelligence gathering devices with sophisticated satellites overlooking various nations, and listening posts with extensive military intelligence that spy and gather so much information on each other. This was evident during the Cold War between the West and East, and has expanded over the centuries to include cyber attacks in many forms.

Cyber attacks utilized by nations are highly sophisticated. Country's utilize their most intelligent and smartest people; giving them tools and technologies to gather as much information possible by any technological means. This process has been going on for many years to prepare nations for defensive cyber attack when a war or action of war takes place on one nation against another.

Technologically advanced nations have created cyber attacks and spying through many of their national security agencies. They provide the policies, guidelines and processes, and recommendations to various agencies within government establishments to protect its' date and infrastructures that are vulnerable to computer attacks. The defensive actions are in place in almost all of these countries. For example, Western countries who are members of NATO, share one strategy in terms of defending their infrastructures from cyber attacks under the umbrella of Nato's Cyber Command and Control Center.

Less developed countries have started to wake up to the existing threats of cyber attacks in past 5 years in a serious manner. They have started to copy what the more advanced nations have done in past 10 years. This is good news, but unfortunately it's just the beginning of a long road in protecting the countries' infrastructures. Acting defensively against a cyber attack is an important step a government in developing countries should undertake. Unfortunately, this task is given to the Information System and Telecommunication authorities of each of the six nations within the Gulf Cooperation Council (GCC), which are considered civilian authorities.

These governmental authorities bureaucracies get together with their counterparts in advanced countries to learn how to protect them from cyber attacks. They were advised, given their limited technological abilities to create special departments such as computer emergency response teams (CERT) to manage any cyber attacks. They were not asked by their counterpart in developed countries to create NATO and other advanced nations when it came to cyber security centers. Why is this? we do not know. But one can guess, that all major information systems and telecommunications vendors and companies selling their hardware or software systems are in advanced countries, and developing countries such as the six GCC countries, and are considered consumers of services and products of technologically advanced nations.

The less you have control over the security of information, the easier it is for many countries to spy, and also for software and hardware companies to expand their businesses and money making machines.

I remember an experience when I was asked by my a government agency to bring in telecommunication encryption devices in order to protect the Ministry of Foreign Affairs from spying and listening in to phone calls and reading emails and messages. The telecommunication providers of hardware and software refused to provide the maximum encryption level software, because the country who invented it, does not allow export outside its' borders. Therefore, you can be a user but not be allowed to be given the encryption keys to encrypt your own. If you try it using the foreign country's hardware and software systems, there is always a back door access and decryption methodology that the company has given to its country government establishments in order to access your systems anytime and from anywhere. So, my advice to the government department was that you do not have a choice except to use the system, and if the government agency wants to deliver a secure message, then it should be done on a face-to-face basis and not to utilize existing technologies, because advanced nations are always listening.

Being defensive is a good thing for less advanced technologically that is at mercy of more advanced nations. These less privileged countries employ people of the advanced countries and pay them huge salaries and benefits, but unfortunately do not have control of their own life's when advanced nations take offensive spying and data collection actions, and many times launch the deadliest worms and viruses in order to cripple these less fortunate countries' infrastructures. Not only that, but advanced nations such as the United States, China, Russia, France, UK, and including Israel, have developed cyber Command Military style organizations. Most of these Cyber command and control centers were formed in the past 5 to 6 years. These Center's intention, is not only to deter and defend their infrastructures, but also to take offensive means by attacking other cyber defenseless nations with planting trap doors and time bombs. These cyber advanced nations have already installed and planted these trapdoors and logic bombs into each other facilities and infrastructures in the case of Cyber Wars, and in order to achieve their agenda.

Trapdoors are basically the means by which a programmer or operator has access in a computer system if needed. This is done by knowing how operating systems of intended computer networks operate. Cyber attackers have acquired required access identification and passwords. While logic bombs are software codes that are embedded in millions of other codes either in applications or networks operating systems. They are activated in a zero time or on command when attacker already has installed a logical time bomb to be activated in future time and on demand. These lethal cyber weapons when activated can cause major damage on country's installations and infrastructures.

Iranian Nuclear Facility & Stuxnet

The first publically known cyber attack on one nation to another nation is Stuxnet. This is a widely reported virus attack and confirmed a work of a nation or group of nations. The virus is written to control speed mechanism control systems which in turn are controlled computers. Stuxnet was launched to damage and slow down Iranian nuclear facilities and prevent Iran from coming close to developing nuclear technology and ultimately nuclear bombs. The virus was installed to control units that control the spinning of the reactors that enrich uranium. Affected sites are the Natanz uranium-enrichment facility. As reported, the virus was a covert operation initiated by the Bush administration to install the virus switches that control these enrichments units, and thereby slow down the overall processes and or sabotage the program. Iran admitted such sabotage and consequently persecuted and punished many people involved in operating the nuclear facility. They were considered spies and working with Western countries. Stuxnet is considered one of the most sophisticated viruses developed. As one closely looks into the structure of the virus code and functionality, it is apparent the worm was developed by an organization that was well funded. It required many man-hours and sophisticated programming. Some reports suggested that it is the work jointly between the United States and Israel.

The virus might have been sent via a computer network or the Internet. In order for it to have any success, it has to be downloaded using an email system with a file attachment containing the virus. It can be also launched, using any storage device and most likely USPs (thump or flash drives), which means, it has to be an internal job that is done by someone within the facility. That is why the Iranian authority when the virus was discovered, had to look inside and do the necessary investigation and eliminate the threat.

Stuxnet is a time bomb virus, infecting switches that control spinning of cylinders that enrich uranium. It is reported that Siemens switches used at the Iranian nuclear facility were already infected by the virus without knowing, and were activated at certain time. The virus is programmed to look for and to aim at frequency-converter drives. These drives control the spinning speed of the centrifuges by altering its speed and ultimately damaging them. While this is done covertly, facility operators will not notice any changes to operational speed shown on monitors, and operations appear to look normal. The virus had one mission which was to slow and damage the centrifuges enrichment controllers. Therefore, it had a limited mission. It cannot spread to other computer devices similar to other well-known viruses, which we will be presented as examples in this book. It is not known if this virus has any fail-safe mechanism or self-destructive code. What is known, is how destructive in disrupting and damaging the industrial infrastructure of a nation is. Stuxnet is credited with achieving its' objective damaging approximately 30% of the centrifuges operational at the nuclear facility thereby reducing Iranian efforts to come close being a nuclear nation.

There are many scenarios as to how the Stuxnet virus got into Siemens's control units. The most likely scenario is the use of a USB drive inserted into the local desktop computer and thereby considered an inside job. Another scenario is an email sent to any staff working at the nuclear facility. By opening an attachment file which contains Stuxnet, the virus was launched. Stuxnet is coded with ha Zero-day exploit, which is known in the Windows operating system. When an attachment file is opened, Stuxnet is programmed to infect the

Windows computer with Step 7 software and SCADA (Supervisory Control and Data Acquisition) PLC (Programming Logic Controller), which is a hardware device controlling centrifuges for any industrial system.

The Stuxnet virus has many layers to attack and it aims at Windows Operating System taking advantage of the zero-day weakness (Windows claims fixes already in place). It targets industrial control systems such as Siemens PCS 7, WinCC and STEP 7 Industrial Software Applications running Windows. This is the first well-known discovery of any malware launched by a nation or group of nations collaborating against another nation. Although, this worm has caused the damage it is intended for, Microsoft managed to know about this weakness of its' software operating system and came out in collaboration with Siemens with right patch, hoping that such fix can stop further hacking. The discovery of the Stuxnet virus was in June 2010 but several reports indicate that the virus launch might have taken place as early as 2009.

It is claimed that Stuxnet is so sophisticated and complicated, that only a nation with advanced technological means could have written the program. The virus is 500KB (half megabyte) of codes, and this is considered very large with written codes within one program. The purpose of this virus is not only to carry out one attack but also multiple attacks simultaneously. The attacks were also reliable knowing well what to target and when. It had the ability to understand well Windows operating systems, applications and weaknesses. Stuxnet is written to exploit vulnerabilities existing in the Windows OS, particularly exploiting the zero-date vulnerability which made it such an easy hacking task. In fact Stuxnet was so advanced in terms of keeping itself stealth and unknown to the attacked nation. It kept doing its' intended job for a long period of time, and for a number of years, until the job was accomplished, Attacked nations realized something was wrong with its' operations in the very late stages after the damage had already taken place.

Stuxnet codes target vulnerabilities in the processing of files and Windows task schedulers as well windows XP. The virus had the ability to carry out multiple attacks. It has a program within a master program to cover a remote exploit using printer spooler subsystems by sending the virus to other peers within the network. This enabled attackers to ensure all vulnerabilities within Windows32 covered, thereby provided ultimate virus attacks known to anyone in cyber technology. There were four Windows zero-day exploits in Stuxnet. One strength of this virus to ensure that no obvious indications of an attack has taken place. There was no memory corruption. It has stealth capabilities which mean the virus is hidden within other programs and cannot be located and only activated with a zero-date is activated. Furthermore, Stuxnet used original signature certification which is required when carrying out any modification or insertion of any executable rootkits programs within the Windows operating system. The attacking nation managed to obtain legitimate certification from authorized companies by Windows. The legitimate certificates were issued by two companies named JMicron and Realtek, and both are based in Taiwan. Only nations with powerful technological means can accomplish this. Not only were the attackers able to obtain knowledge of all necessary vulnerabilities of a well-known operating system such as Windows which basically operates 90 percent of personal computers, and used in many industrial and large complex computing environments. It is also obvious by exploiting these vulnerabilities and using them in writing Stuxnet codes, meaning the nation would have in its' arsenal other stealthy viruses and be ready to be launched in future attacks. It would be a scary scenario to many nations to comprehend, and take stock of this fact when procuring and implementing a software system or an application within the computing environment, that such systems already have been dissected and witnessed vulnerability within it. It was discovered by the same nation who invented it, and the codes written in worms and viruses can be leashed upon any nation when desired.

Stuxnet did not only accomplish its' mission of damaging nuclear uranium enrichment cylinders to a large extent that slowed down considerably the Iranian ability to produce any potential nuclear capabilities, it also enabled nations to initiate the attack (which is always denied by any nation accused by such attack) to have mirror operations of the facility operation and to take control remotely over plant's activities. Stuxnet was able to report to two command and control centers in Malaysia and Denmark, and to report in a mirror style environment to attackers. The virus was written in such a smart way, that not only was it doing the job it was written for, but it presented a lie or different reality to those technicians and operators working in the nuclear plant. Stuxnet would show them that the operation was normal and that there was nothing out of the ordinary when it was the opposite. The ability of the virus to issue reports of wrong status of centerfusion rotation levels was unbelievable. Stuxnet managed to change this rotation in various higher and lower speeds, allowing it to behave crazy and out of control, and thereby causing it to spin at a random pace and ultimately damaging it. But reports to plant's operators showing centrifuges were at normal speed. The best part of this Stuxnet virus, was that it allowed the attacker nations to keep updated with the virus with further instructions and new codes remotely. This process showing sophistication in nation cyber attacks, will be a subject for further investigations and discussions.

This is easily done when spy agencies can install viruses and worms in your computer devices or phones and copy everything you type or listen to every call within a certain distance. Listening and monitoring technologies are done through powerful listening posts, relay microwaves, and satellite technologies, and many other tools. Many cyber technologists discount this possibility given the difficulties of remotely controlling industrial facilities of another nation. Due to this cyber attack and other attacks with Iran, the country decided to invest billions of dollars into its own cyber warfare program. Many nations realized this and have created their own Cyber Centers by investing billions of dollars with the hope to defend and protect its' industrial and other vital infrastructures.

Although, Windows and other American technology products are not permitted to sell to Iran, it is not known how they got them into the plant, and how the Iranian would trust using it in a major secret and vital industrial complex where the world is watching and major industrial powers namely the United States and Israel are amongst many nations in the world who want to stop it from becoming a nuclear nation.

Georgia and Estonia & DDoS

Estonia is considered one the most wired country in Eastern Europe. The use of the internet in private and governmental agencies and populations ranked as advanced as in the United States and South Korea. One day many servers in this country were flooded with requests in using the DDoS (Distributed Denial of Services) types of virus affected many services such as online banking, government websites and utility services. They were not accessible by the public and out of order. Although DDos attacks are considered somehow benign in nature as they only cause servers hosting websites flooded and jammed with requests coming through emails or just basic access requests. When memory and storage capacities of websites exceeded it, the system will not function and shutdown until operators get involved and resolve this situation. Most of these cyber attacks are done through robotic types, preprogrammed instructions, or programs written by hackers and installed on computers that are used for as cyber attacks. DDos viruses are programmed to hit certain operating programs. One major virus used by these robotic computers is the use of Botnet virus. The Botnet virus which has the DDoS style of cyber attacks and can be loaded into these robotic computers, instructed to attack other computers. If your computer is infected with botnet you would know it, by noticing your computer is not running its' usual speed and is taking a longer time than usual to run. This is where the worm is typically activated as system is turned on and it is taking over your operating system and sending all types of requests to other targeted computers and slowing down machines. They however can cause so much disturbance to services and can shut down websites and accesses to computer networks, where many online services are dependent on such as bank, airlines, travel agencies, and others.

So many computers were affected and the number would be in the thousands, and in fact a major bank in Estonia was so badly hit that the bank had to suspend services. This is in addition to the communication network systems which was disrupted. Estonia blamed Russia, especially when they traced back the cyber attacks by the machines they originated from, it was discovered that they were coming from Russian territory. Russia as usual denied such action and blamed it on activists and rogue hackers. Same problems happened in Georgia when conflict erupted with Russia, and similar DDos attacks in Estonia disrupted many websites and communication infrastructures. Due to DDos attacks on Estonia and Georgia-Russia Communication Systems were affected and impacted the country's ability to communicate within its' border and abroad. NATO stepped in and had to create and adapt for its nations members a new policy called NATO Cyber Defense Policy. It also established in 2008 the Cyber Defense Center in Tallinn, the capital of Estonia. NATO's cyber center regular exercises with all countries' partners to simulate and find better ways to protect members' infrastructures against cyber threats and attacks. They have large numbers of specialists from different countries involved in the testing and improving Cyber Defense Policy adapted. For the record, NATO itself was attacked by hackers who were able to block its' website and deny using email access for several days.

NATO became aggressive in combating cyber threats. In the NATO summit in Lisbon all NATO members agreed to a new security concept and framework, and came up with a new cyber defense polity to counter any hostile attacks, and take immediate protection actions. NATO also created alongside established Computer Incident Response Center and Cooperative Cyber-Defense Center of Excellence in Tallinn, to provide training in cyber threat and protection fields.

Israel attack on Syrian nuclear reactor

The purpose of the attack on the Syrian nuclear reactor was to shut down Syria's radar and anti aircraft defenses by using latest methods of jamming technology. In jamming the defenses of the Syrian military equipment, Israeli aircrafts were able to penetrate Syrian's airspace unnoticed.

No one knows what type of worms was used to infect the Syrian's computer system, mainly in the Command and Control Center that controls radars and anti aircraft defenses. It is reported that Syrian pilots never took off with their aircraft, to fight the Israeli pilots as they were not show on any radar. The attack on the nuclear reactor was extremely successful. Many speculate that it's an early version of the Stoxtnet virus, and the same one that is used on Iranian reactors to slow down and damage nuclear center fusion enrichment cylinders. How Israel managed to launch the virus is also a mystery, but many analysts do not dispute that Israel has probably the capability to launch the virus through the net although Syria is well known for its' less advanced computer infrastructure. Also, there is the possibility of using the USP stick manually and thereby this becomes an insider job. Either way, the success of the attack demonstrates the ability of a nation with great knowledge, in using its' most powerful technologies to launch Wars using cyber attacks and paving the way to complete the job without even spilling blood or suffering any causalities. Israel managed to destroy 23 (SAM) networks in addition to bombing on the ground 80 Syrian aircraft. The impact on Syria was devastating, and a great humiliation, as this nation used to pride itself as being the only Arab country that could stand up to Israel.

Middle East: Flame, Dugu & DDoS

New types of viruses now targeting countries are DDOS (Distributed Denial of Service) which are similar in its' damage abilities to the ones launched in Georgia and Estonia. Both the Flame and Dugu viruses were also reported to be the work of nations because of their extreme technical capabilities and similarity in code writing to Stuxnet. They are used by Cyber Attackers for spying purposes. They are powerful and stealth in nature. Attacked nations would not know of their existence for many years. Middle Eastern countries who were targeted, did not report any attack, but the news was reported internationally. Many GCC countries, which are considered wealthy suffered the most. Fingers point towards the USA and Israel as the collaborating nation in writing the codes of these two viruses. The two viruses are similar in size to Stuxnet however, with a different objective in mind. They are launched to collect intelligent and sensitive information on the industrial and government facilities in Middle Eastern countries.

Dugu: It was discovered in 2011, and the name came about because few of its' files containing the prefix DQ. The main purpose is to spy and collect intelligent information on targets. In order to keep the worm stealth and not unknown is to write its' codes of not causing any harm to the target's information base, and computing records. The delivery mechanism of the Duqu warm is through spearhead phishing attacks. Targets would receive emails with attached files. The target client is enticed to open the word document attachment to an email. The email is well written in a language that is familiar to the recipient, without raising any suspicion. When the sent word document is opened, the worm is launched and immediately exploits the kernel vulnerability of the Windows operating system, mainly the file win32.sys. The worm will remain active and in executable form, even when the word processing file is closed. It stays in memory and keeps working in the background, installing itself as a backdoor avenue for the attacker. In order to install itself as an executable file in rootkits of the operating system, when it is installed it must have authority to do so, and must use a valid certificate as a digital signatory. Apparently, this was the digital signatory authority which was also stolen similar to Stuxnet. Companies where the theft took place were based in Taipei, Taiwan. When the worm takes control of the computer system, it starts to collect information on the system in an extremely detailed way, down to the keystrokes. It is so advanced as a spying techniques, that it can capture screen shots, collect passwords, and search for files. Many other functions that we do not know could include spying on all connecting networked computers, and spreading the worm to other computers within the networked facility, similar to Stuxnet. With regards to reporting, the Duqu worm can send all collected information to servers located in many other countries via any telecommunication means, it has been assigned for, and in this can probably utilize the wide world internet. Once this nation that has the capability to write such a complex and powerful worm is discovered and anti-viruses and intrusion-detection methods employed to stop it, there are always ways to tweak the worm and add more functionality and utilize new vulnerabilities, to be launched again. I presume this worm and many others already available, not only privately held within the industrial countries intelligent communities and military commands, but also on the black market, and for the right price it can be acquired for any malicious act against the intended targets.

Flame: Recent reports of cyber attacks on Aramco Saudi Arabia and Rasgas Qatar were attributed to a worm called Flame. Both of these companies are major national oil and gas producing companies for their respected countries. Flame was so infectious, that it impacted thousands of computers. It took targeted companies many days and weeks to clean up and bring back computing operations to a state of normality. Ultimate damage is not fully known, as these government-owned companies are not allowed to issue press release or publically admit that was a target of cyber attack. There was financial damage for certain but also loss of reputation for not sustaining computing operations for companies. It is not know if this attack was generated locally or from a foreign source. However, it is also well known that these two companies have invested heavily in their computing and telecommunications infrastructures, and installed the required firewall, intrusion-detection programs, and updated anti-viruses. With all the human and financial resources they have on hand, they could not stop the virus attack on their systems. Flame attacks for example on Aramco impacted approximately 30,000 computers operating within the company. Similar large numbers of Flame infection happened with Qatar Rasgas. It is not clear who initiated this Flame virus and which country it belongs to. Iran was one of those countries initially mentioned as the culprit due to its' disputes with Saudi Arabia, but we will not know for sure. However, given Flame code's written sophistication, it is likely such a worm was written by a technologically advanced nation.

Flame like other sophisticated viruses exploit the Windows operating systems. When it was discovered in 2012, cyber experts found this   code so extensive and complex, it resembled a code written in Stuxnet. However, the size of the code was found to be of greater multiple in size to Stuxnet, which proves the fact is written by an advanced nation, and could be from the same country or countries who produced Stuxnet.

The objective of launching Flame, is to collect massive amounts of information in a mega-data style on targeted companies. The data to be downloaded from the computing centers and personal computers of the two companies reported, was so large, that Flame codes contained functionality of compressing, encryption and transmitting all over to cyber attackers' locations internationally. However, the full capabilities of the Flame worm is not yet known, but there is a certain similarity to Duqu especially in its' spying functionality. Flame has more sophistication than Duqu. It can record any audio and Skype conversations in addition to recording keyboard activities and traffic. Flame was able to exploit every vulnerability there is the Windows operating systems. Once the machine is infected by Flame, it is basically under the thump of the attacker and can do anything remotely using backdoor commands that are set up in the rootkits of the operating system. Similar to other viruses, the cyber attacker will need the authorized digital signatory of the operating system in order to have the authority to make changes to executable files. This ability to obtain the private key to allow the cyber attacker to act as the authorized signatory and carry out the necessary downloading of files into the kernel rootkits, requires to a major cryptographic ability to copy such a signature because these private keys are typically encrypted and only the author of the installed operating system and associated files are allowed to carry any addition or amendment to the existing files in the main operating system of any computer system. The other option which is similar to other viruses is to acquire the original digital signatory authorization from clone companies based overseas such as Taiwan.

It is apparent that such launching of sophisticated viruses and worms intended for spying and collecting information purposes are targeting specific countries in the Middle East. We all know that Iran is the ultimate target, but we never expected Saudi Arabia and Qatar to be on the list. As well one would assume due to net interconnectivity that such worms first attacked Iran and this was a reported fact, and from there it spread to other neighboring countries such as Saudi Arabia and Qatar.

Objectives of cyber attackers are still not fully known but the functionalities of Dugu and Flame indicate that they were for spying and collecting information. The cyber attackers are clever and smart to disguise their attack through email files written in such good English or the language of the country involved. In this case Arabic for both companies in Arabic countries such as Saudi Arabia which are considered two of the richest countries throughout the GCC. Dugu and Flame were launched through emails. The cyber attacker emails would show sophistication and subject knowledge in the area they are targeting such as Oil and Gas, Financial, Education, or Health Care. So, a targeted email address would contain a file or a link and when it is opened the worm is launched, causing damage in accordance to its' programmed codes. If a link is sent rather than an attached file to an email, then this link can be directed to attack a person to a login page, specifically written and designed to give certain information that would lead to access victim's email and the downloading of files, emails, and any other types of information per worm's coded instructions. In using an email approach, which is called Spear Phishing, it can be written is a normal and industry standard so that the person attacked would not even suspect it, and would seriously think it was coming from a legitimate source. If the cyber attackers are intelligent, they would use special emails with special reference wording and subject matters either financial, investment, education, or health care, and others with semantics and terms used within the specific industry.

Cyber security officials both at the FBI and FireEye (Cyber Company) identified recent attacks on executives at many companies using a software program called Tor. This program which is used by cyber attackers to log into victims' email accounts and route them through the internet around the globe, thereby making the process of tracking and finding where it came from would prove to be very difficult for law enforcement officials. These are sophisticated attacks and can be carried out by individuals and most likely organized groups in many countries with intelligent abilities of knowing well what to do in terms of writing such emails in native languages, and with subject knowledge, then sending them across to industries and executives, and launching cyber attacks. Flame and Dugu were discovered and patches and fixes to the Windows operating systems were included, however this does not mean that source codes of these types of worms cannot be modified and avoid any detection system in place, and continue to be launched and achieve intelligent purposes.

DDoS: The Distributed Denial of Service, is basically what its' name means. The Cyber attacker disables the target machine and by a virus denies service provided to its' client. These types of viruses are so common these days, that they are available for hire or buy either through the net or black market. It has been used by many on individuals and also on a group bases. Within the Middle East, we heard of many such attacks, and potentially dangerous ones that would come from groups with political agendas or grievances against countries aiming to launch attacks on country's institutions. Examples of such attacks are the Israeli hackers attack on the Saudi Stock Exchange (Tadawul). The attack shut down the Saudi stock exchange's website. Other attacks included hacking into the websites of many other organizations within the Saudi Kingdom, such as the one they took place on the Saudi Medical records of all students. Given such brazen attacks between Israel and Saudi Arabia, where one country might have the ability to launch an offensive attack, it seems that Saudi Arabia through its' own hired hackers managed to launch an attack on Israel. An example of this is when a Saudi hacker named OxOmar managed to bring down the Tel Aviv Stock Exchange and El Al airline websites. They also obtained the credit card numbers of many Israeli citizens and managed to publish them on the net. These cyber attacks, such as the attacks between Israel and its' neighboring Arab nations, is continuing in regular fashion and in many forms, mostly with regards to DDoS types of attacks. However, the more serious of worms and viruses that have spying and stealth capabilities will not be known between these nations and also from other countries coming into Middle Eastern countries.

I would expect the numbers of attacks to accelerate in the coming months and years, and in fact if the year 2014 is an indicator of number of attacks just reported in the media, the large numbers of these attacks will never be mentioned in the public due to loss of face and reputation. We will see multifold cyber attacks in the year 2015 and beyond.

Shutting Down Water System in USA

It has been reported in 2011 that a utility water pump in central Illinois was shut down due to remote hacking. This cyber attack was the first known attack reported in the United States' media. It is claimed that the perpetrators or hackers are foreign, and targeting the US industrial systems. There is further information on how the attackers managed to obtain access to the facility. One explanation is that they managed to obtain credentials with authorization means in accessing the computer network. No one knows for sure if it was done by an inside job or through obtaining user access via an online hacking. In any type of access obtained, hackers were able to enter the network's grid without flagging a notice and thereby shutting down the water facility. Many utility companies use the Supervisory Control and Data Acquisition (SCADA) systems. These are specialized software programs that control industrial and facility processes. Vulnerability with SCADA came about with the application of on-line internet in which many of these industrial facilities require remote monitoring and diagnoses which make them pray for hackers.

A similar attack took place in 2003 by a worm named the Slammer, and was intended to attack the SCADA power grid's network system. Electric power was taken out in eight states in the North East which affected millions. As a result of these attacks within the United States and around the world on power and utility grid systems, many nations and mainly the United States asked through the regulatory forms of all utility companies and many of them privately, to install, adapt, and operate appropriate cyber security systems, with the hope that such cyber security systems, protocols, and procedures would protect this vital and sensitive infrastructure. This does not mean that these grid systems are safe from cyber attacks just because they have security measures, they are far from it. The basic fact is because these systems must be connected through the company intranet (which is a network system just operating within the company to connect its' computer and network systems and employees) and the internet (which is an open network to everyone outside the company). A hacker can easily penetrate the company's intranet because it is connected to the worldwide internet, and thereby cause all intended damage. The level of damage depends very much on the type of worm implanted and or sent out via the internet. The majority of these attacks on power grids will come through logic bombs that are already implanted into computer network systems, and software systems operating the power grids such as the SCADA one. The fact that logic bombs are already in many switching systems' networks controlling power grids operations are considered a scary proposition and scenario for any country.

We have given above many examples of cyber attacks by nations who invested heavily in cyber wars on other nations. Investments in terms of human brain and financial resources that are mainly used under cover and never announced publically. Nations' cyber attacks we illustrated as examples are reported in the media, but there also are many, that we do not know about and many nations and its' media will not be able to report them. They are almost all under the cover of some entities or groups but never naming a particular country or a governmental agency.

The main issue here is what a nation can do to protect its' infrastructure, and how nations that have technological muscles are working heavily involved in cyber offense competitive nations thereby weaken them in order to achieve certain agenda. Cyber attacks are occurring on a regular basis amongst the big super powers. Cyber security is regularly on the discussion agenda of many of the G20 countries. They meet on a regular basis discussing how to reduce cyber attacks. However, they will not reveal to each other their clandestine undercover cyber operations , and even if they get caught and evidences are produced to the guilty party, denial is always around the corner. The simplest answer by the guilty country is that if an attack is generated within and from its' border on another country's facility, these attackers or hackers are rogue ones and are not part of the government. Both the USA and China are at the center of such controversy in recent times with attacks generated from each side.

However, as reported the denial is the only response to be given by an official spokesman in order to escape responsibility and further embarrassment. Cyber security is such a serious matter between the two nations that either would not allow companies working in computing and communications networking systems to bid or get any contracts with respected government entities. Many large Chinese telecommunication and computing products and technologies are prohibited to enter into any tender or contract with any United States governmental agency for fear of stealing and transferring, and more seriously damaging the country's sensitive data. Similarly, China will not allow American computer and telecommunication companies to filter into the echelon of the Chinese government establishments for fear of spying. Recently, China has taken an even harder approach in changing its' policy to only install locally hardware of computers and communications gears with software that are modified and cleansed from any security threats at its' government agencies.

A few years back, the United States had many cyber command centers at different military units such as Army, Navy and Air force. Recently, they were joined under one US Cyber Command. Similarly, China in 2002 announced the establishment of the Cyber Warfare Unit, meanwhile in 2003 Russia created FAPSI (Federal Commission for Government Communications and Information). There are around 20 or more nations which have such centers including France, Israel, Iran, South Korea, India, Pakistan, and many others. They all have defensive and offensive capabilities of attacking and planting cyber weapons mainly trapdoors and logic bombs in each other's main computing infrastructures.

Although some of these centers have carried out and will carry out cyber espionage and other intelligence information gathering requirements, few have left cyber espionage to other intelligence agencies to comply with local regulations and rules. It is an easy progressive process to move from a defense cyber approach to an offensive one, if a country devotes resources either human or financial. Worms and viruses are not only available for a good price from the black market, it is easy for any country to recruit and train programmers and cyber security specialists who are familiar in creating worms and viruses that are used in an offensive manner against nations.

The Syrian Electronic Army (SEA)

This organization belongs to the Syrian government with a mission to attack and hack into its' enemy website using existing internet networks and telecommunication mediums. SEA has been successful in shutting down many websites of different government organizations not only in the Middle East but also in Europe and the United States. Recent reports show that they were successful in launching their latest hacking techniques on the websites of large media organizations such as Britain's The Independent, the New York Daily News, the New York Times, the Huffington Post, and the Guardian. The hacking message is so clear on the screen users, which states that you have been hacked by the SEA, and to stop publishing negative reports on Syria and Syria's Civil War. The SEA group also have been successful in launching cyber attacks on government sites in the Middle East, such as Qatar Foundation, in the State of Qatar, because it supported freedom fighters against existing the Syrian government.

The question is how did they do it? and are they doing it from inside Syrian territory? and are they really of Syrian nationality? This question is very hard to answer given clandestine cyber operations of many nations. It is hard to prove a cyber attack from one country against another. In the case of SEA attacks, we know for sure given its' name, it is coming from Syrian government, but if you ask them, they will deny these attacks from government, and this SEA is a group of sympathizing hackers to the Syrian's cause. What will we make of this? One clear answer is not where they are located even though they call them the Syrian Electronic Army. They can be anywhere in the world. As long as the group have access to sophisticated computer systems, with network ability, and ISPs addresses that can be diverted from one country to another without given its' signature being from initiated location attaching country, they will be able to hack to any computing facility if they have advanced hacking abilities. One can assume there is no stopping this group to carry out their attacks. Another major factor, is that if this group indeed has technical and financial support from the Syrian government, then we be assured they will acquire all technical capabilities helping them in their hacking missions.

In order to successfully achieve any cyber attack, there is always the need for qualified programmers who are able to write programming codes that can penetrate the most advanced cyber defenses created by the attacked nation. I would assume Syria and Syrian citizens are not as technically advanced as Western Countries. In fact, I would assume knowing Syrian educational and technological infrastructures, they are not capable of carrying out such sophisticated hacking in shutting down many websites around the globe, and causing damage to data and of course causing financial harm to many organizations. So, the argument goes to the fact that SEA must have sophisticated programmers from nationalities other than Syrian. It is not strange these days to recruit many of these talented programmers and pay them huge sums of money to undertake these hacking missions.

If Syria as a country in the midst of a civil war with limited technological and financial resources, and in which it is divided where in major parts it is not in control of its' government but under the control of many rebellious groups. The Syrian government has a grudge against so many countries, especially the western allies who are intending to topple Bashar Assad's government. Creating a group such as the SEA with the mission to attack the websites of many organizations in the developed and developing countries by a government so under attack and a country in ruins, just imagine what an advanced country or even a developing country with massive financial and technological skills can do to another country when it comes to a cyber war.

Chapter Three
Corporate Cyber Attacks

Frequently and on a regular basis we hear and read many stories of cyber attacks on big corporations and companies in many countries. Many cyber attacks are taking place regularly but are not reported for fear of bad publicity and reputation, however when it is reported then it is for legal reasoning.

These cyber attacks are mainly on industrial and big corporations. The aim is to disrupt, steal files and data, or to bring down the financial structure of the target. There are many examples of cyber attacks, and we will pick the most famous ones widely reported and will have major impact, and we can illustrate potential damages caused.

International Monetary Fund (IMF)

The International Monetary Fund (IMF) had a major attack on its computer networks. So far no one has claimed responsibility. The purpose was to steal economic data including files, emails, and any other relevant information that were stored on organization's major computer mainframes and personal computers. It is apparent that the attacker installed a virus designed to allow the intruder to have a digital presence. The IMF's computer network contains economic, social, and financial data relevant to every country in the world. There are types of information that are considered highly classified due to the nature of the Fund in providing financial and economical assistance to many countries in terms of long terms. Hackers managed to download all types of information through obtaining access authorization including employees' passwords and emails. The attack was so serious that the Federal Bureau of Investigation (FBI) was called in to investigate.

The World Bank which is another major financial and political organization in Washington DC, had its' computer network infected with the virus. A possible scenario is existing on-line link and sharing of information between sister organizations. The World Bank is similar to the IMF. It also provides financial, social, and economic assistance to countries through loans and grants. The World Bank had to disconnect its' mainframe computer from the IMF following the discovery of a virus for fear of virus spreading. The details of IMF cyber attack magnitude of damage is not known and was not reported. Hackers managed to get away with valuable information of many countries helping the cyber attacker's country, and if not from any particular country, but a group intended to make financial gain in selling the countries' sensitive information on the black market. Certainly such information will be valuable and will have a large price tag.

In using Spear Phishing technique, hackers managed to launch the IMF's virus. This cyber technique is common amongst sophisticated hackers. It utilizes a written code to be placed in a file and attached to emails that are sent to IMF's staff. When emails with attached files are opened, the virus is launched and will spread itself throughout the network into other computers carrying its' destructive mission as it is instructed. This type of virus must have been written by a sophisticated party with a higher agenda, and not by a small type of hacker. Many sources indicated that such hacking is connected to a foreign government, but this is hard to prove. Even if a government agency traces a cyber attack to its' origin in a foreign land, it will find out it is either initiated from a public source in a public location coming from either a university campus, an individual home, or group of people meeting in a coffee shop with free public wifi. Regardless of who originated its' sophistication and intention, one can conclude it has to be a work of a foreign government. The IMF managed to clean up its' network system with help of its' IT team and assistance from cyber security firms, and law enforcement authorities. However, as they recovered files and relevant information from the organization backup system, hackers intentions have been achieved, and in this case, the thief already got away with his prize, and the only option for the owner of the prize is to replace it with a similar one. Cleaning up an entire computing environment is not an easy job, let along backing up all data and files. Such processes are time consuming and not prone to having virus stealth within the system, and awaiting further instruction. They are known advanced hacking sophistications. We cannot waive any potential future attacks, if it has happened once, make sure it will happen again.

Sony

Sony International USA witnessed one of biggest cyber attacks on any corporation in our modern time. Its' last attack was in 2012 on the Sony's Playstation network system which was shut down by hackers. Approximately, 100 million accounts with personal information stored on the company's computer system were compromised. What this cyber attack meant is not only loss of confidence in its security system, but hackers' ability to penetrate and download all types of sensitive information. Sony did not just lose financially, it also lost its' reputation and the confidence of its loyal customers.

Two years later in 2014 after the Sony Playstation cyber attack, this new attack turned out to be more damaging. Sony Entertainment is based in Los Angeles, California. It produces major files and blockbuster movies. This attack on the computing environment of the company was considered so severe and major, not only was the public alarmed, but the world took notice. Even the President of United States of America had to comment on seriousness of this cyber attack and the damage it caused to a major international company such as Sony.

Prior to this second cyber attack and following the first attack on the Sony Playstation network, the Sony Corporation spent large sums of money and employed human resources to heighten its' cyber security measures including hiring major cyber security firms, to ensure all of its computing environment is secure. It installed firewall, anti-viruses, and intrusion-detection measures to counter different types of viruses and worms known to the industry. Sony believed with this strength in computing security, cyber attacks are distant possibilities. It turned out to be a wrong assumption and this new cyber attack is listed in history books as the worst attack on any public corporation.

Every major public report in the media pointed fingers on North Korea following the federal authority's statement. The reason for the attack is that Sony was about to release a new movie called "Interview", about the assassination of North Korea's president. A comical movie where two journalists recruited by the CIA have a mission going to North Korea in attempt to achieve an impossible goal of an assassination while conducting an interview with country's president of North Korea.

Federal authorities indicated Sony's virus was written with a trace of North Korean language in it and therefore it must be initiated by Korea with a motive to stop release of this new movie made by Sony harming the reputation of country and its' president. North Korea named as a culprit, was constantly mentioned in media and in statements by US government officials. There was no concrete proof from the government's cyber intelligence agencies and reliable resources in North Korea that might have done it, but there will be a culprit to be named. North Korea is for now considered the only suspect of the attack. One can conclude when reading these stories in major newspapers to be factual, but we know that there is more to these reports. What is the damage that was done to Sony? Early reports state that cyber attackers managed to extract valuable classified company staff personal information including salaries, health care files, passwords, social security numbers, and even how much bonuses were given. Furthermore, attackers also managed to download the newest movies before they were released which caused future financial losses. Attackers are not just satisfied with downloading all of the company's files, movies, and other types of information, they have written a virus with instructions to wipe out clean all storage devices, and shut down the company's computing environment.

A group called itself Guardian of Peace with a hash tag (#GOP) claimed responsibility. No one heard of this anonymous name before, and to which country they belonged. There are many theories as to how the worm was delivered and launched. In understanding the work of worms and viruses, we will need to use telecommunication means to deliver them: a worm or a virus, and how to trace to its' origin. One will assume that Sony's security measures will prevent any worm to penetrate it, and thereby a second guess scenario is assume it only can be launched as an inside job. A similar Stuxnet launch occurred at the Iranian nuclear facility. Certain reports mentioned that a disgruntled employee managed to insert the worm using a flash card. This is the most likely scenario. However other media reports kept North Korea's story alive giving increasing publicity to the movie the "Interview". Sony was careful not to blame North Korea by name before getting all the right facts while investigating into the incident still going forward. Facts will come out as more information will be released and uncovered.

Sony Corporation's complete computing environment was shut down and the company resorted to manual operations and office paperwork. Sony could not even start again by rebooting the system. The worm is still not identified by either cyber expert or the FBI assigned to the case. Apparently, it is not work of an individual but seriously organized with support by highly technical and financial organizations belonging to country. Therefore, when the name #GOP announced as the hacker with the assumption that it is a group supported by North Korea. It was not surprising news to the cyber security community.

North Korea has some capabilities, and with the help of the Russians and the Chinese, it is possible that with over 700 cyber programmers that are not necessarily stationed in North Korea but could be in China or Russia, with the ability to launch cyber attacks all over the world. The government of North Korea denied such an attack and blamed it on sympathizers and supporters of the country against the intention of Sony to launch the movie which was causing extreme embarrassment to the President of North Korea. We will be hearing more about the story as it will evolved in the near future. One story which came up in newspapers following the disclosure of the attack was that the group initiated it from a hotel lobby in Thailand which has a public wifi. This story immediately died and there was no proof of it. We all know in order to attack the protected computing facility especially at Sony, it would have to be from a sophisticated environment not from a hotel lobby. It is surprising that until the writing of this book we have not heard or read any more news about on this matter. The movie "The Interview" was launched and DVD copies were distributed all over the world. We all knew it was a comic movie with a scenario only Hollywood could think of. The main issue here is about Sony hacking, and why it could not stop the attack given all cyber protection measures in place.

In recent cases of cyber attacks the intention varies mostly in stealing files, various sensitive information and disruption to computing network environments. The motive behind such action is either malicious or financial, but the Sony attack intention is not only stealing files, downloading, and publishing them, but in destroying all information stored on drives by wiping it clean. This type of action is considered serious and the most elaborate of any virus or worms launched by any hacking group. Until the writing of this book, nationality of #GOP (Guardian of Peace) which claimed responsibility for the hacking is not revealed. All fingers are aimed to North Korea as this group has made the threat by demanding that the new film "the Interview" depicting an assassination of Kim Jung-Un, the President of North Korea. The country denied it is behind the attack as a typical denial of any country involved in a nation hacking. The only comment from North Korea was that the group hackers are sympathetic to North Korea's case.

Sony for sure managed to back up all necessary information and many large companies have duplicated back up facilities to restore operations in times of disasters, and in this hacking case, it was a major disaster. We only hope that when the backup was taking place that programs and applications running such back up were not also copied. It is within that possibility that the worm or virus is stealth and awaiting future activation instructions to come alive and be launched following the restoration of computing operations at Sony. It is understood that without computers and especially with large corporations such as Sony they would be unproductive, time consuming, and frustrating for employees and company officials having their emails made public and could not get back to computing operations immediately. I am certain the cyber security company or companies who were hired to clean up the infection of the worm are working diligently in restoring computing operations as soon as possible. One major issue is that how we can make sure that such a worm is not still dormant on personal computers given that that the virus has not been identified and we do not have an anti-virus tool kit for it. So, the fastest way to restart the operation is to install new computers and a network system from scratch, which could be expensive, with the hope that the back-up system the company has is not infected and therefore we do not have a repeat of this sad and devastating episode. The United States government and even the president of United States of America, Mr. Obama has come out publically and labeled the attack as a type of cyber war, which is unusual and unprecedented coming from an American president. In a public news appearance he assured the American people that United States will take appropriate action in the times of its' choosing. North Korea on other hand, responded publically and denied strongly that the attack had come from its country and people. North Korea requested the United States to produce any evidence it has, and requested that a joint team be established, in order to exchange and work jointly on this matter. The NSA and FBI did not disclose any detailed information on the attackers, but briefed the government officials and the President of the strong evidence they collected and apparently they have "as they say" pointed to North Korea as the originator of such attacks. They claim North Korea has used similar worms and viruses of cyber attacks on South Korea where many computers' data were wiped out after downloading information, and these computers have become inoperable. Thereby, the conclusion drawn by government officials is that Sony's cyber attack was the work of North Korea.

As this incident occurred during the writing of this book as it was evolving, the Sony attack is the first obvious attack made allegedly by a country named which was North Korea against a large media company based in the USA, Sony. The damage according to President Obama's press conference was very damaging financially to the company, and politically to the

USA. The Sony CEO confirmed on a televised interview that the attack could not be stopped even with the strongest firewall and cyber security the company employed. The CEO emphasized that the company recruited very specialized cyber security people and in fact were working closely with the authorities especially the FBI, following previous attacks. But this particular attack in which the FBI and the President of the United States clearly named another country which was North Korea of the attack, and that the U.S. would take appropriate action against the attacker. The attack is classified by the president as an act of war, but this was downgraded to an act of cyber espionage. North Korea as a typical nation involved in any attack would deny and it did so vehemently and asked the United States for evidence and clarification with regards to the country's involvement in the attack. The United States meanwhile is asking China and requesting that the Chinese government block any cyber attacks from North Korea. This is a very strange request given the fact the relationship between the two countries has been strained in this sphere following the United States accusation of China being responsible for the cyber attack on U.S. companies, and the government of America named five high ranking Chinese military officials by names and splashed their pictures all over the media, which caused embarrassment to China, and strained the relationship. Now the U.S. is asking for cooperation from China to block any networking access to North Korea, given that North Korean telecommunication network is handled by the Chinese network and must go through its' telecommunication network system to the outside world. The company in China handling all internet traffic of North Korea is the China United Network Communications Group, better known as China Unicom. Therefore, this is why I believe that North Korea would not have been able to attack all along although it has all the reason to do so giving Sony's intention to release the movie "Interview" which satirized the assassination of a sitting president, which was reported was as a bad choice by the entertainment company. As this story was evolving, we witnessed a high alert by many companies and of course countries, with regards to how easy it is to shut down the operation of one company infrastructure, and in this case, Sony's computer networks and all of its' computers files and data were wiped completely out after downloading these files, emails, and other data in the hard drives of the computers. There were approximately 100 terabytes of the company data in the public now for all to see which caused such severe embarrassment to all, not only to the executives of Sony but all employees and families as personal emails were exchanged and many conversations of movie stars and others have became public. The worm used in the attack was so powerful that the computers were not operable anymore, or booted up. The cost of the attack according to the Sony CEO was so huge that he could not place the monetary value. The cost of the movie the Interview which is causing all this fuss, cost the company approximately 75 million dollars, but the financial damage could run much higher, over 500 million dollars, not counting the political damage to a country such as the United States which values freedom of the press, against any types of censorship, and in this case, Sony claimed that by not showing the movie because the movie theaters around the country refused to show the movie for fear of being attacked themselves, which is another reason that has not been logical. However, the company according to the CEO was intent on proceeding with showing the movie to the population within the United States through other means such as digital video or online on demand movies.

The United States is planning to take the offensive towards cyber attacks against the infrastructure of North Korea as the President of USA stated in his news conference. Unfortunately, any attack will only involve the use of DDOS (distributed denial of service) types of attacks where the internet network of North Korea will be bombarded with pockets of data, that is so massive, the internet network within the country will be partially if not totally shut down. North Korea has a very limited internet protocol address (1024) compared to a small city within the United States which might have thousands of such protocol addresses. Similar attacks have taken place with one nation against another, like the ones on Estonia and Georgia in 2007 and 2009. The North Korean internet is very low in terms of penetration as the nation is considered to have one of the lowest penetration rates in the world, and is less connected internet wise not like the Unites States which is the most internet and wired nation in the world. Thus, North Korea is what we considered an intranet networked nation, which is basically the network within the country controlled by a state owned company and the low network the country has is directed through this agency via a state owned communication setup within China. So, all internet traffic is routed through the Chinese National Network System. No one really knows for a fact what caused this network disruption failure, is it coming from the North Korean government itself trying to block its' internet from the outside world fearful of potential attack from United States government or groups associated with the government, and by the way the United States will not be directly involved in a cyber attack, but usually groups associated with the government, and this is the game all governments around the world play, where they use groups financed by their governments to carry out their cyber wars or cyber espionage against other nations. The facts and more of them will come out in near future and more will be revealed. The biggest story to be revealed and many cyber specialists are anxious and waiting to learn is the type of worm and details of the codes writing that caused such massive hacking damage to Sony. This attack was so devastating that the worm written by highly sophisticated programmers that were able to penetrate the highest secure network in any organization or company. The other news we will be awaiting to learn is if this is an inside job or a job carried out through using the world wide web. An inside job is the most likely option as such an attack would have been difficult to carry out over the internet given its' sophistication and the types of damage that the different files with the worm must attach to and reveal and further destroy and wipe out all data and basically disable the computer networks and anything attached to it.

As the story of Sony is reviewed and we will hear more about it as facts are revealed by the attack and what type of worm was used that devastated the computer networks of Sony. With this cyber attack if finally proven, it was generated by North Korea and the country's sponsored group, the GOP (Guardian of Peace) will be unprecedented because this cyber attack has come from a country with the lowest penetration of internet and technological advancements although the country is a nuclear nation but the level of computing and networking is considered low compared to other nations in advanced and developing nations, and one would wonder what if any nation with the technological muscles can do if it has the real intention to cause harm using the cyber war against another nation with a political and financial grudge. These potential possibilities are real and happening around us without having them reported in the media. Potentially, one country that is affected financially by another country. Also, let us say what is going on now with the oil prices sliding across from the high of 110 dollars per barrel to less than 60 dollars within a few weeks or months, as these financial losses to many oil producing countries such as Russia and others will feel for their economic loss in the coming months and will these start to blame other nations from the lower oil prices, and potential retaliation can be in order, and therefore we do not know what the future will hold, but ultimately we know that nations will resort to all means to protect their national interest and considered economic losses and future revenues of their nation as an act of war, and the easiest way to counter attack is to use the cyber war through the world wide network system and other means of electronic espionage to alter the course of event within the country accused of such act of financial loss and force the country to change policies.

In addition to Sony, there is other reported news of cyber attacks on corporations within the USA in the media, but there is not much detailed information revealed by investigations by the FBI and other law authorities across the United States. Therefore not much is information released except the ones by the public relations departments in press releases. For example, a serious corporate cyber attack took place on the number two American health insurer, Anthem Incorporated. It was reported that 80 million of records have been stolen from a data base belonging to the company. It is believed that it is one of the worst attacks on a health insurance company. The data stolen is personal information related to consumers and employees. It is so sophisticated and claimed that it could not be done except by another country with sophisticated cyber technology. The United States is naming China as usual. These stolen records can be valuable on the black market, but even though they are medical records, the information obtained from the data base could also be included with other sensitive information. Of course Anthem was able to report the cyber attack incident immediately due to fear of legal litigations, other companies in similar situations typically would not.

The company contacted the FBI and claimed that the security breach on its' IT system had been fixed and that security was restored. One would wonder if there was any cyber security before this incident happened. We assume there were extensive security measures taken given the latest hacking on corporate America, and even with this there was no stopping to the cyber hacking into one of the biggest corporations in the United States.

Similarly, Home Depot was attacked and 53 million email addresses were stolen. The company Target also was hit by a cyber attack and 70 million customers records were stolen.
Although the Sony cyber attack was considered the most brazen and damaging, using one of the most sophisticated worms written in attacking a major corporation. These types of cyber attacks will continue as long as advanced hackers have the technical ability to carry them out. Therefore, we will hear more of such news in coming months and years, some of them will be reported and others will not.

Chapter Four
Hacking Threats

The level of hacking differs depending on the level of seriousness. Hackers therefore can be classified in terms of their skills. The more advanced the hackers skills are, the more serious the level of cyber attacks are. Hackers that are involved in Nations Wars typically are considered advanced hackers with very sophisticated programming knowledge to be able to write the virus or worm codes creating the necessary backdoor or Trojan horse attacks. The low skilled hackers typically those who use remote access or commands in Spear Phishing emails and hack into the websites of an entity. Most of these hacking codes are commercially available for a price, and also with low level programming skills, anyone can hack into websites and emails. Then there is the lowest of all hacking, which is driven by commercial products that are available in the market, and with low prices such as skimmers and tools that can steal your credit card information. This level of hacking does not require any technical skills and criminals use them as tools to assist them in their hacking process.

The fact of the matter is that hackers are so well equipped not only in technology knowledge but they also posses the means and tools to hack into anything either public or private. For them there is no defense out there to stop them if they are persistent. Therefore, in order to understand hacking we must understand the threat level that comes from hacking. Threats in computer terms is to expose the existing vulnerability in either hardware or software systems. Hackers know that when they find this vulnerability, there is no stopping their hacking into anything, and therefore security as we know it does not exist. Therefore, no one is safe from a hacker with the right skills and tools. Smaller organizations belonging to smaller countries as in the GCC countries, would surely not be safe given the limited defensive resources they have to stop a hacker not only penetrating the system and compromising its' security but also to keep in hacking, and staying within the system through different backdoors generated by the written virus codes without organizations or countries realizing it.

One of the main reasons for many entities either governmental or private companies located in small countries not having cyber defense capabilities against advance hacking, is the high cost to install the appropriate cyber security measures. Even with all the spending on maintaining cyber security measures such as firewalls and anti-viruses, there is no guarantee that valuable organization's assets are protected from attacks. Hackers will have the technical ability to break in and take away everything if they are seeking anything. It is that simple.

Organizations would spend money on cyber security to mitigate risk and reduce it to an acceptable level against cyber attacks. Top management looks at IT operations as a cost center not a revenue generating business unit. IT departments always put up higher budgets every year and a majority of the cost goes into ensuing updates and implementing security measures including firewalls, detection-intrusion methods, antivirus, incident response, and patch management, security awareness, training, amongst others. These are costly matters and we will always see top management and especially finance departments who would weigh in cost as to how minimize cost against the potential risk of a cyber attack that might never happen. CIO and IT managers look at the computer environment protection as an important issue and cost as irrelevant while Finance managers would like to have cost reduction regardless and weigh risk against cost. Finance departments would look at cost of risk and if it is worthwhile, to spend so much money in providing cyber security, and if organization's assets are worth spending a huge sum of money. This is the dilemma that occurs on a daily basis amongst many of the companies and organizations in many developing countries.

Constant Threats

Organizations and various entities of all types and sizes are vulnerable to cyber attacks. Just when they are considered safe by installing all the security measures mentioned earlier, new vulnerabilities come out due to software upgrades or new applications. In those millions of codes that applications contain, the possibility of discovering one flaw that can be exploited is always there for a hacker. Many hackers always look for certain vulnerabilities hidden in these programming codes, and today many software vendors along with hardware vendors in the silicon valley are determined to batch up all these vulnerabilities and to declare zero-date free. Zero-date is the most famous vulnerability found in many applications which are exploited by many hackers.

The advancements in computing, networking, and communication technologies have made the average layman confused and at the same time alarmed. Given the constant news coming across the media about hacking and cyber threats, and that many companies and government entities were hacked and their information and assets compromised, has made many decision makers worry and even give up on the concept of having to install proper anti-virus software programs or patch their system and to ensure all applications are screened and virus free. However, many others have become concerned and that is why many high technology companies are now employing many cyber experts to provide the necessary knowledge and expertise to support their client base.

Hackers are the most knowledgeable about computing and networking environments more than any other person working in the computing environment. They maintain offensive capabilities in penetrating any system. They usually have to accumulate so much knowledge about the targeted organization, and to know every detail there is socially and technically. While the typical IT organizational environment is always on the defensive, and takes pride in employing the latest security measures assuring top management of providing the necessary security environment to organization's operations. The applications of computing and networking technologies within an organization have become nowadays a must. Every organization either private or public is working towards implementing the latest technologies enabling operational smoothness and convenience to its clients and customers not only locally, but also internationally. You will not find one organization that does not have a website, a Facebook, or a twitter account. These tools have become necessary as social media, and they are indispensable in people's love of mobility. Organizations not taking social media seriously are considered out of touch with modern times in communication with the general public. Therefore, security and vulnerability have become an issue, and the more technology any organization employs the more vulnerable for hacking. The problem with this is that the IT defensive mode is always reactionary and fixing whatever vulnerability occurred, and if local expertise is not available to do so, it relies on the vendor who supplied the product to provide the necessary patches, and also updates to ensure that their products are safe. A good opportunity for vendors is to sell more of its' products and provide additional products that are believed to enhance organizational security measures. They will marvel at the fact that they are innovative and must sell products that are safe and secure. These vendors must also bring to the market updated software and new products in order to ensure their leadership in the market place, and to compete in a fierce and competitive environment, and in doing so, they are always in a rush to push into the market new technological products that are alpha and beta tested, but unfortunately they are filled with vulnerabilities, and in which hackers typically will find them and exploit them. We will discuss these vendor products in more detail in coming chapters. There were studies that confirm with every 10,000 lines of programming codes, there is at least one vulnerability. Therefore, imagine if there are millions of written codes in one software application of an operating system, database, or just a business application. These many hardware and software technologies are employed in various vital infrastructures and in each country, from power utilities to banking. They are filled with vulnerabilities making the hackers' job easy to penetrate them. The most famous example, is the zero-date vulnerability found in the Microsoft Windows 7 operating system. The operating system has therefore approximately 50 million lines of codes and thus imagine the number of vulnerabilities it must contain and in which can be exploited by hackers.

No Fear

Hackers depending on their level of technical hacking can avoid being caught. Countries across the globe are racing to bring out laws and regulations to persecute and control hackers, and put them out of business. However, as we can see and read in various media that hackers and especially nations or stated supported hackers always get away with their hacking actions. There are so many cases of hackers that have been caught and brought to justice, but the sentences imposed on them are so light, many of them come back into business as soon as they are out of legal troubles.

Hackers with advanced knowledge can hack into any system remotely from any country in the world. They can use proxy servers and bounce their accesses from one server to another, thereby making it so hard for law enforcement to follow them and actually determine for sure from where an attack originated. Furthermore, hackers and I mean really advanced hackers can wipe out their traces of attacks after achieving their hacking objectives. The worm or virus that launched will include certain commands to erase and delete any trace of the hacking, and therefore organizations would never find out if the source, and when they find out they were hacked it would be too late as the damage is done. Well, depending on the intention of the hackers, some will include command instruction not only wiping out the hacking trace but also deleting everything on the system, and in fact making all computing environment's inoperative. Those hackers are so fearless and can work with impunity across countries. By the time law enforcements find them, they have already moved on and gone.

Three levels of hacking

1. hackers working with governments in launching cyber attacks particularly in spying and nations' wars with other nations. These types of hackers are working for nation states. They not only utilize huge inventory of worms and viruses accumulated over the years within the intelligence communities across USA, Europe, Russia China, and other nations, they also maintain code writing and programming abilities. They have a highly technical generation of skilled people that are recruited and funded. It is estimated that North Korea which does not come even closer to the technological skills of nation hacking to many advanced countries listed above, as have reported over 700 full time dedicated hackers under its' military and intelligence establishments. They are located not only in North Korea but across the globe to carry out the hacking mandate. The most common type of hacking with nations sponsored is the use of backdoor worms or viruses thereby maintaining prolonged stealth access and acquiring the desired data and other spying activities indicated in the coded instructions.

Backdoors are executable programs installed in the roots of the operating systems, and they can auto start and restore itself. Many backdoors viruses are often written for Windows operating system given existing vulnerabilities. However, other operating systems such as Mac OS, Unix, and Linux are also used in writing the backdoor code instructions.

2. Hackers utilizing Social Engineering coupled with technology to hack into corporations and other entities. The most common is Spearhead Phishing remotely targeting organizations' emails and conning websites. Other hackers who are able to utilize available technologies and tools such as skimmers and other physical devices to steal for example credit cards..etc. to achieve their objectives, and these hacktivists and cyber or techno-criminals are the most common hackers. The main drive of these hackers is financial and achieving maximum economic objectives. As the products' technologies of these tools is upgraded, the utilization of them becomes widespread and global. The group devoted to these elementary and basic hacking are typically gangs and groups of people organized to carry out the hacking. The duration of the hack might not last for a long time, similar to a theft of a house where a thief would steal and run away and ensure not to get caught. Hackers using these tools are not going to stay stealth and it would be a hit and run style of hacking hoping that they would not be caught in the long run. Federal authorities have an easier job going after them due to forensic evidences they leave behind.

3. Hackers who utilize many software toolkits under their arsenals. Many of them are traditional such as stack and heap overflow, cross-site scripting (XSS), SQL-Injection, and file format bugs. These toolkits are typically required to write virus or worm codes and commands. The expertise required in writing the codes is in programming language knowledge in

Linux and Java operating systems as they are common now. The required knowledge by hackers with regards to these traditional code writing is probably so high tech that many hackers do not have the time or the skills to acquire them, and therefore are left to state sponsored hackers with financial and training means to provide such skills. However, many hackers with technical knowledge but not necessarily high code writing skills in any of the above mentioned language, can be as effective in hacking and achieving results. Every hacker in the hacking community knows how easy it is to acquire various viruses and worms without even having the knowledge of code writing. These viruses and worms are available to purchase on the black market with the right price. The most famous viruses available in the market are the Botnet. They are used to create DDos (Disrupted Denial of Service) attacks. Others utilizing the Zero-Date ("0"-day) vulnerability which is so common in many software applications and operating systems where few batches are available for fixes. The cost of purchasing these or joining the group who have them and constantly updated them, will require the purchaser to pay a hefty amount depending on the level of virus effectiveness. However, imagine with certain programming skills and having these viruses available from the black market, any hacker can basically change certain source code within this program and turn the virus into a more lethal one to hack into any organization or entity. This has now become an open field for many criminals and terrorists organizations, and we have seen so many examples of DDos attacks in recent months, and many of them reported and others have not. In fact, just having these viruses available to anyone with financial and political powers to obtain, create uncertain world where any individual, or group of organized people, or even state sponsored hackers, can infiltrate many organizations and in many countries and create havoc we do not need, and might start wars amongst nations.

The percentage ratio of type three hacking is much more higher than the other two. We read and hear various media reports about them. It does not mean the nation hacking which is the first type is as high and keep constantly going on and in a stealth way where the attacked does not know they are spied on and hacked. They are basically not reported enough in the press and therefore what we read and hear in the media is the other two types of hacking and those are targeted against individuals and corporations.

Hacking using type two is much easier , with a click of a mouse from anywhere in the world, either sitting in a closed room or in an open public cafe in a hotel in the middle of a city, the hacker can use a public wifi network which is offered for free in many establishments in sending an email with an attachment containing the virus. In today's world where we are all connected through an email system and with wide spread mobility with advance emailing systems and other types of technologies, the target is always on and can be tempted to open email attachment out of curiosity or ignorance, in which a worm or a virus can be launched. Virus or worm code writers posses high technical skills in programming. They either work for governments or a well financed organizations. Of course there are skillful solo programmers that would write worm code after discovering certain vulnerabilities in either the operating system or a software application, and thereby the experiment of launching it as a challenge or other purposes. Also, there is the black market and websites that hackers know well and can share such hacking codes and techniques, and place a price on them in terms of sales and economic gain.

Why do they Hack and How?

Also we should define different types of threats that are out there which make many organizations vulnerable to cyber attacks. There are hackers that are motivated to utilize their intellectual curiosity and there are others with political agendas. There are also nation states who would like to spy and steal secrets from other nations, and there are cyber criminals who can utilize technically gifted individuals or a groups of people in writing for viruses them and worms for the purpose of stealing and causing major damage to data and computer networks, again mostly for economic gains and a political agenda.

The lowest of all the hacking technologies is the use of existing commercial products in stealing money or information. The most famous of all these is the use of Skimmers. These little machines are used by any individuals with criminal intent. They are mobile and easy to use. Skimmers can be of a simple design or are more sophisticated one. They are used to swipe your credit card when you go shopping or dine in a restaurant. All your valuable information stored either on the magnetic strip of the chip of the credit or plastic card will be read by these machines and stored in a computer to be used at a later stage by the hackers with the software tools they have in their toolkits arsenal.

The most advanced of all skimmers are the one used on ATM machines and in particular next or above the card slot.

Customers insert the ATM cards into them thinking they belong to the bank, and not knowing that all information stored on their cards' chips are wirelessly sent to the hackers' computer. Banks recently realized this scam and opted to change such ATM card slots by making sure the protection of card insertion is covered. However, with all the camera and other sophisticated tools available with the banks, they are still having more and more ATM cyber attacks, as criminals are finding new advancement in commercially available products available to them on the market.

Many sophisticated techno-criminals resort to advanced hacking by using advanced software systems that are commercially available on the black market. One can search and find them on the internet. They offer a convenient means of hacking either physical or otherwise, but less and less requirements of technical programming skills. These low skilled criminals basically utilize whatever is available in the market and they are either solo individuals or organized criminal groups taking advantage of the existing weaknesses in many systems or other global operations. However, most of these types of hackings are discovered through normal operational auditing, and they are easily traced back to criminals. The smart ones however can shut down their operations and leave in no time, never getting caught.

Some hackers also use guess work to steal user identifications and passwords, and mainly passwords, which are not easy to obtain. While these types of hackers have an agenda to obtain passwords of targets and get to their emails and files when they access website addresses. Guessing passwords requires a level of intelligence and lots of guess work. Typically, if you type a wrong password into a website, using either Google or Microsoft, you are required to re-enter the correct password, and if hackers keep trying it will end up after a number of trials by asking you if you would like to reset the password using the functionality of "forgot password" provided by the website server. Thereby, providing confidential information you have entered when the email address was set up from the start such as birth date, mother name, nick name, city where were you born, and other personal information, a new password will be given and hackers then take control of your email address and have full access to the account. These types of hackers usually have done their due diligence and homework in finding out all the information required about the target especially if the attacked person is a public figure or a famous celebrity and well-known personality. Most of their private information is available in public social media, and can be researched. Therefore, their guess work starts, when they hit the jack pot, they are in the email address reading all emails, files, notes, and downloading everything including pictures. This is what happened to many famous personalities especially in the U.S., where their pictures were downloaded and became public. Furthermore, when hackers obtain the email passwords of their targets, they can even impersonate the owner's email address, and send emails to all friends and colleagues requesting money or asking for favors thereby causing financial loss to people who trusted emails or messages coming from addresses and names that are familiar and they have known for a long time and trusted. The attacked person would not know if his email address is compromised until he gets a call or an email from a known associate informing him of the email sent by him asking for money as an example. This type of simple hacking is so widespread and is one of the largest and most well known forms of hacking. Wealthy countries and especially in the GCC countries, receive hundreds and even thousands every week of such impersonating emails, and the only solution to fix it, if it is found out that the email address is compromised, is to change the password address and start all over with the hope that you have backed up all your important files or pictures.

The "Forward" functionality provided by the website servers allows customers to redirect incoming mails to one account and send a copy of any email to another account. Hackers only need to use this forwarding functionality by resetting the attacked email to send every copy of email, message, or a picture to the hackers' email account. This way the target does not know that the account is hacked and compromised. This process can go on for a long time until the attacked person changes their password. Therefore, it is always recommended for one change to the password more frequently providing the necessary protection to personal and business information stored on a daily basis in the email address. People in many facets of daily business life and businesses depend so much on emails. So just imagine how easy it is to impersonate email addresses. Hackers are doing it on a daily bases, and this has become a big business for criminal groups who are bent on extortion and stealing personal and business information for economic reasons. Also, spy agencies are using them extensively. However, with spy agencies they would use more sophisticated virus codes, rather than just guess work using social engineering, in accessing email address accounts. The danger of this type of hacking is that many people are taking the matter lightly not knowing the damage and implications of having their email accounts hacked into or impersonated. Just imagine if someone obtained your email account and now is sending emails, messages, pictures, and other information to person, or persons, and to the world with wrong information and misleading letters and pictures. How damaging would this be to the person's financial well being, in addition to his security and reputation. There are many horrific examples of these hackings happening to them, and I am included, when someone managed to obtain my password, and sent out group emails to all of my contacts and they were in the hundred requesting an amount to be wired overseas because they said I was traveling and in bad shape after having all of my possessions stolen. The clever thing about those hackers, is that they did not request a big amount, just a few thousand of dollars, to make it more convincing. A close friend with financial means who knew me well, knew that I travel quite often on business trips and that I was in no need of sending such money, another friend who also knew me well, knew I would not ask for such money, and that I am an experienced traveler and such an issue never happens especially when your have communication with you banks to wire you money and still have relatives that can do the job or even friends. This case could happen to anyone. It is so wide spread and common, and the most damaging cyber attacks occur on personal email accounts that touch the person's daily life.

The point above illustrates how easy it is to learn to hack with simple tools and a certain knowledge level, which is now available on the net and easy to research by, understanding and learning the concept within few hours or days with little effort. Most criminal gangs across the world and mainly in Eastern European countries, have resorted to this type of hacking, and have enough financial resources to buy most advanced computing. They can impersonate thousands of email accounts across the globe and send hundreds of emails to millions of people, knowing that if one percent will respond to these attacks, it will net them millions and billions of dollars. Recent news from the nation of Tokyo for example is that in 2014, the country witnessed the highest hacking attacks that exceeded 64 million attacks. The financial sector lost approximately over 1 billion dollars, not including the compromise to personal accounts and emails.

As for the nations using the cyber attacks against another nation, there is noticed an increase in such attacks over the past two years, and it has been accelerating at a fast pace. Leaders of the Western World have had to act and set up coordinated efforts to try to put forward certain policies and guidelines to implement at their intelligence agencies, with the hope to mitigate the risk of having their vital sectors attacked. Of course, this is a tug of cyber war between major industrial countries, where we see on one side the United States and European countries, and on the other side Russia and China. Then we have smaller developing nations who are trying to get into this "Super Power Cyber Nations" Club, and are developing their own cyber weapon arsenals. They are also storing as many worms and viruses that are available in the hacking communities, and they are also training and hiring the best programmers and code writers that can write the most lethal of codes that can cause the greatest destruction to a vital sector of any country. The most famous of these cyber nations attacks are one used recently in many countries and are reported heavily such as the Stuxnet attack on the Iranian nuclear facility, or the Dugu worm launched against the Iranians in spying on their citizens, and then we have the Flame Worm, which is also used in cyber espionage. Dugu is more sophisticated in spy activities where all audio and other media phone conversations such as Skype are listened to.

These worms are developed by a group of highly intelligent programmers and code writers that are heavily financed and sponsored by state owned countries. The budgeting for these groups or organizations that belong to intelligence agencies is unlimited and highly classified. As their work is classified, their plans and strategies are held in secret. In fact, when the European and American countries meet and discuss strategies regarding their coordinated efforts to counter attack the face of enemy cyber attacks, they would not share their cyber technologies in detail to the point of how many worms and viruses and other cyber weapons they have, this scenario is similar to discussing how many nuclear bombs or other conventional weapons each country maintains. Cyber worms and viruses have been classified in military terms as weapons.

Types of Viruses, and Worms used

The three major types of viruses are classified and defined based on their characteristics and the job their codes are written to accomplish. However there are so many techniques and tools hackers use to get the job done, but let us get some definition with regards these viruses and worms:

A) The Virus is a program attached to a host program or a file, and only works and is activated when this program or the file is opened. Its' mission is to replicate itself based upon the intention of the written code, it can copy, delete, or transfer data.

B) The Worm is a code written to be installed into the programs and applications, and based on its' mission, it can do anything it wants. Mainly it changes the host programs or applications while moving into the computer system.

These viruses and worms either come as a Trojan Horse or backdoor capabilities. The Trojan Horse is a name well known in the battle field where the attacker hides its' intention and activates the attack based on a timely order. This is the same, where a virus code is written by a sophisticated programmer but hidden inside other host programs. The code is then activated and triggered when the main host program is initiated and activated. While the Backdoor type is a worm and can stay stealth for a long period of time as its' function is not to destroy or cause any flags or alarms to the attacked target, but to allow the hackers to come back to any system updated to follow up on further instruction.

The specifics of their actions varies depending on the codes written. The viruses in general are similar to human viruses where they attack the computer operating systems and applications and then spread out to other computers through the net or copies software from one machine to another. Trojan viruses and malwares are more specific viruses intended to carry forward specific tasks when certain triggers exploiting certain vulnerabilities are exposed in the operating systems or applications such as the Zero Dates in the Windows operating system. The task is triggered and instruction within the codes written will then be activated. They do not contaminate another computer unless the files containing such viruses are copied and implemented into an operating system or an application where the worm is written for causing the necessary infection.

Although, we should not hang onto the definition but we can safely group them into worms and viruses. We hear of so many types and names that are coming out in media, however when a programmer writes a hacking program filled with codes that contain either 10 or 1000 instruction lines, we understand that the objective is to launch this code and achieve the end result. You might call this a virus or a worm depending on the specific task these codes are written for.

Chapter Five
Corporate Vulnerability

In recent weeks and months, a different type of attack targeted firms in many countries either financial, oil, gas, educational, healthcare and pharmaceutical companies amongst many. The purpose is to steal corporate secrets, or classified and sensitive information in order to acquire financial advantages especially in cases such as the banks. Recent examples of such attacks are in health care and drug companies. The attackers were capable of acquiring valuable information and selling them in the open market. Cyber attacks take the form of stealing passwords of accounts and acquiring addresses and then downloading email files of employees working in the company. The number of firms attacked are in the hundreds according to FireEye, a major cyber consulting firm handling major cyber threats and breaches, including the recent Sony attack. Companies listed on the stock market are mandated to report to the US Security and exchange Commission, and share legal matters, mergers. and maintain research and development files. Therefore, any emails and files attached used by employees would be a good target for hackers, and in which will give them financial and economic advantages when they have such information to be sold later to competitors in the black market.

These attacks are basically in the form of stealing files and not causing any damage either to files, computer systems or networks. We always hear and read in the media that the Chinese and specifically the Chinese Government is the culprit. Reasoning is to gain competitive advantage, economically, and to be competitive in the world market against other nations. By cyber hacking and stealing without large financial investment, the Chinese and any other nations would save time and efforts on research and development. However, as always these nations when they get accused would vehemently deny such cyber hacking.

It is true that other nations do acquire such information through the cyber hacking, but also companies do hacking themselves. They do not necessarily do it in a direct way but it is so easy in these times to hire hackers and pay them for the hacking job. FireEye and other cyber security firms indicated cyber attackers are home grown or based in Europe given the use of English which shows their language sophistication. The use of such language is particularly important in having attached files to emails sent to targeted people using spear phishing technique, and not raising any suspicion regarding incoming mails.

US Government & Technology Companies

Recently it is reported that there is a dispute between the US government and the American technology companies with regards to encryption, especially with the revelation of Snowden about the government spying and keeping metadata stored through all listening and monitoring techniques. American technology companies have always been cooperating with intelligence agencies of the United States, and thereby it would not be surprising that they would cave in and provide the necessary access to encryption method companies such as Apple for its iPhone or Google employed in their commercial products. The United States would and will get their wish either with or without the cooperation of these American technology giants. The United States has the technical means through its' massive technical human resources and infusion of huge capital expenditures to utilize their intelligence agencies to create required decryption technologies, which it has been doing for the past years going back to World War II. Currently, the US government is stock piling massive numbers of zero day vulnerabilities, some have been already used, and others to be used in future nations wars or whenever it is required. These Zero Day vulnerabilities are weaknesses in the software commercial applications which are developed by the American technology giants. Although, there are batches to fix these vulnerabilities, these software applications are always updated with new versions, and there are millions of written codes, which make it easy for hackers to discover new vulnerabilities to be exposed for future hacking.

High Technology companies recruit many hackers to discover any vulnerabilities in their software technologies and applications, and pay hackers large sums of money to ensure that they are not vulnerable to hacking. The United States Government on other hand also employs hackers and highly sophisticated techniques to find out any Zero Day or other vulnerabilities in technology products and to ensure they have first hand advantage to spy or install the necessary Trojan and backdoor viruses.

The United States government has confirmed recently the increase in cyber hacking on corporate America and that cyber security must be on the top of any discussion agenda amongst nations. Obama has given a recent speech to

Congress bringing the awareness of cyber threats not only on American companies but as a national security issue. Furthermore, the American president has been coordinating globally with world leaders particularly with Nato members and other G7 nations to put in place a cyber deterrence policy. According to recent news from the American media, the White House will make serious decisions with regards to encryption techniques currently that are used by American technology companies in their commercial products. It is so well known in the cyber world that any encryption technique developed by an American company is quickly decrypted by US intelligence agencies. Meanwhile, The US government has made it difficult for any nation to acquire them. A formal US approval must be given not only by the White House but also from the US congress, which is not easy to acquire. Many nations try to provide to their international customers a feeling of comfort in the fact that they are employing encryption technologies approved by the US or European governments, and that their systems and data are secured. Of course, this is far from the truth. The fact is that every encryption technology sold overseas, the US or by European governments are already decrypted and therefore can and will spy, listen, and monitor all communications that they come across.

Corporate valuable assets protection: Information and money?

Many corporations have major issues when it comes to their valuable information and data set. They are so dependent on them that without the computing environment, it is close to impossible to manage manually. The heartbeat of any corporation is the vitality and availability of its' computing environment. The system has to be functional and on-line. When it is compromised and hacked, and in these many ways brought down like the case of Sony attack, then this corporations not only suffer major financial losses, but ultimately loss of data stored with information loss of its' millions of its' customers and products. Furthermore, the loss of intellectual to attackers cannot be measured in the loss of money alone but time and efforts.

Hacking and intrusion in small and large companies has become a daily and weekly event and should not be surprising to anyone. If we hear a report in the media about any hacking or intrusion on a company, typically it is coming from an inside whistle blower, or an attacker wishing to reveal the attack to the media or a third party for the purpose of publicity. We see this is happening quite often in the past few years and increasingly in years 2013-14, and we will be hearing of many more cyber attacks in coming years. Many corporations are not reporting these attacks due to the loss of face and prestige, or worse, the fear of legal litigations by its' clients and customers. Therefore, not all attacks discovered by these corporations are reported. Even if such reporting has to be done given the fact many corporations are publicly traded companies, and will not have to report financial and information losses. The reports coming out of company's public relation department is so massive that it does not contain all the relevant facts, and when any cyber attack is revealed, the reader receives misleading messages, which is a border lie.

The highly advanced and technically based hackers usually employ stealth methods in hacking. What this means is that no traces are left following the cyber attack, and in fact such attacks are not even noticed, and these advance hackers will probably still be inside the system and have their backdoor access whenever they want. This is a scary scenario to any corporation. These corporations are in a catch 22. Even if they do employ the latest firewalls, intrusion-detection, and anti-viruses systems, they are always on the defensive. While sophisticated and highly technical hackers have the means and toolkits to find new vulnerabilities in various systems such as operating, networking, database, and other connected devices, hackers are able to create required codes and launch virus and worms. It is a vicious cycle and as long as there is an agenda being financial, political, social, or otherwise, this vicious cycle will continue for the coming years, and for sure will increase. Not only corporations are on their feet to work out the best strategy and plans to have the highest level of cyber security, but also nations have started to take notice, especially when their vital industries and infrastructures which are operated and controlled by these corporations have been hacked and compromised. They are working now in concert to create a strong cyber strategy or update current ones, however, they are always will be on the defensive and the vicious cycle of cyber war will continue.

Prevent & Restore

Bringing back any hacked or compromised computer and information systems' operations to normality would involve many steps and processes. They include preventive and restoration effective such as token, firewalls, intrusion-protection, anti-viruses, and backup systems. They are most prevalent in any operational restoration to any company that is hit by cyber attack. We will discuss these security measures in more details.

a) The Corporate Token

RSA is one of the well-known companies that produce and sell its' Secure ID products to many organizations and corporations around the globe. A corporation can provide data security to its' employee using the authentication process. An employee or user must have two things to access the corporate system and to have the data security either receiving, sending, or accessing corporate websites and systems. First, they must have a private or personal key or a PIN, and this is must be private and kept secret only for the user. Second, they must have a physical device known as token that can display six digit numbers every sixty seconds as soon as a private personal key is entered into it. This number is then used to enter into the web page presented to the user when accessing the system along with user identification and password.

This token is an algorithm developed by three mathematicians, where their first letters of their names are the initial of the RSA and name of the company. The RSA became the standard encryption tool for many corporations who seriously take cyber security threats. The token can be used for encrypting online shopping, banking, emails, massages, and files. There are other tokens beside RSA developed by competing companies. A number of similar tokens employed by many private and government agencies ElGamal keys, such as DSA keys, and ECDSA key, amongst others in the market. However, RSA is considered the most popular and it has set the standard for token in the corporate world today.

The authentication process that is employed in the token is based on complex encryption and decryption methods. Even with the user identification and passwords that are typically used to access corporate sites, users have to chose secret numbers that are kept confidential between users and system operators. Even with such high level technological protection against hacking, RSA was even compromised and hackers managed to decrypt messages and emails sent via the individual users to others including attached files contained in such email systems. The sophistication of the attack on RSA did not stop there, the attackers manage to heighten their accesses and obtain passwords stored in the system and also valid administrative passwords which means accessing all numbers entered into the system from the tokens, and therefore no need for any physical device to generate these numbers.

This type of token is used by many companies as a means to protect users who are connected to computer network systems and utilizes the telecommunication medium. Transmitted data over the net is encrypted and thereby, only the end user with its own use of public keys within the system can open the email system with all attached files. The corporate token has generated another layer of security to its' users and corporate date usage. The popularity of the token did not go unnoticed as hackers figured the weaknesses of the algorithm used in the token and there were several reports of hacking into the network system with the token being used and thereby emails of many users were compromised.

Hackers managed to compromise the RSA secure system by sending random phishing emails to the specific users containing a file with spreadsheet that had the code or virus to take advantage of zero-day vulnerability in the Adobe Flash application. This virus allowed the hacker to install a remote administrative tool in the operating system.

It is not determined who was behind such an attack and major compromises to the most secure corporate tool invented yet. Recent reports that an attack was carried out on American defense contractors, such as Lockheed that extensively uses the token. The United States government pointed the fingers at the Chinese but no one knows the user who was behind this intrusion on the RSA token. With all of these reported weaknesses and other disadvantages of using the token, corporations intend to utilize this technology and feel safe in providing and maintaining their data transmission across the network, and minimize cyber attacks.

In general, the majority of these tokens can provide the necessary protection and security in transmitting email, messages, and files across the network to other users, as corporations are encouraged to use them and required to provide the necessary training to its' staff on the usage and maintenance of these tokens for the protection of the corporation valuable assets, which is its' data.

b) Firewalls, and Intrusion-detection systems

Many corporations resort to implementing firewalls and intrusion-detection systems to protect its' valuable data stored in their computer systems. These cyber protection systems are basically computer systems that stand between the penetrator/hacker and the intended system in the cyber attacking world. These systems are software programs, tools, and kits that are installed into one or more computer systems where all messages, emails, and their attachments, and any other computing and networking activities that come across the main system must first go through. All communications especially across the world wide web must pass through the firewall and intrusion-detection as a front line defense first, and then they get filtered through these screening programs which are basically a dictionary of words, messages, and sentences that are most familiar with the hacking world. The most popular of these dictionary of firewalls are the ones used by telecommunication carriers. With the use of any word that is linked to sex for example, the user will get a message that access to this website is blocked and denied. Many developing countries are using such firewalls to stop its' citizens from accessing sex websites. If there is no firewall or intrusion-detection programs set up on the servers, and this server is connected to the internet, as all servers are located at almost every company, this server will be scanned within seconds by hackers looking for vulnerabilities to cyber attacks. Many companies will see hundreds and even thousands of attacks, and most of them are done automatically by programmed machines and servers dedicated to do the job. These machines are so sophisticated. They are set up to send spearhead phishing with emails and attachments containing all types of worms and viruses. This is how dangerous the situation is if a server is not loaded with the firewall, intrusion-detection programs, anti-viruses, and filtering techniques.

The flaw with the firewalls and intrusion-detection software systems is that they are based on an index mechanism or algorithm with signature base identifying all the viruses and known worms. Any infiltration through words or spam messages must match wording or messages stored in the index and this index and signature base algorithm will be flagged, therefore they are constantly updated with new worms and viruses signatures. Except if the wording and other means of accesses using certain names do not match the index, the algorithm will have a certain level of artificial intelligence recognition recognizing them and predicting if the request is benign or not. They are designed to block anyone with an agenda to hack into the system. Intelligent and advanced hackers figured out how the index system and signature base algorithm work. Advanced hackers can rewrite the source code with less effort and bypass these protection systems. It is assumed that firewall and intrusion-detection systems can protect the network system up to 90 percent, and this is a good percentage, but you only need one cyber attack to bring down the system, and to have a 10 percent vulnerability in an operating system such as Microsoft Windows 7 which is so inviting to hackers to take advantage of and hack any system out there.

However, constant updating of firewalls and intrusion-detection programs are necessary and must be done by any corporation to minimize any attack. There are many companies that can provide firewalls and intrusion-detection systems commercially. The use of sophisticated and almost comprehensive indexes, and highly intelligent software systems can provide the necessary protection, but continuous update and highly vigilant staff looking at all possible flags raised by the firewalls when an attack occurs is an important process to have.

c) Anti-virus Programs

The use of anti-viruses by almost every corporation around the world has become a necessity to counter any cyber hacking attack, and to clean up the computer system when such an attack happens. It is not that easy when viruses and worms are still within the system and in stealth ways. The way anti-viruses work is that the companies who created these anti-viruses also created signatures of all the worms and viruses known to mankind. These are digital signatures and they regularly when anti-viruses activate, scan for these digital signatures and either stop or clean up any virus trying to enter or are already there within the system. Therefore, entities must keep regular updates as new and more powerful and stealth viruses and worms are created and launched.

Computer viruses are also like human viruses where some viruses can mutate in human. Hackers can also escape the trap of virus digital signature in the anti-virus program by changing part of the virus code or instruction, thereby creating a variant needed to escape detection by any anti-virus program. The well known viruses and worms discovered such as Stuxnet, Duqu, and Flame, have different variants, and companies always update their anti-viruses with these variant signatures. The anti-viruses can do the job of flagging in a regular and automatic basis of cyber attacks, and identify what type of action should be taken. However, even with these anti-viruses, a sophisticated and advanced attacker would not be stopped, and this goes for those intelligence agencies across the world who have the technical skills and tools to penetrate anti-viruses programs and avoid signature traps entering the system to achieve its objective.

d) Back UP Systems

The most common restoration mechanism for the data and files stored in any computer system is bringing them back operation on-line from a backup system. Almost all corporations have such a backup system depending on its' size, capabilities, and how critical-mission operations they are? The bigger the corporation, the bigger the size of the backup system. Of course technology of back up has changed over the past 10-15 years. The latest technology is the Cloud backup system, which is not only used for individual users but different sizes of corporations. The mission-critical operation are those companies that cannot afford to go down one minute. These corporations are classified as banks, airlines, stock markets, and many similar operations that constantly have to be online 24/7.

The backup systems can range from a simple redundant storage device that is located within the same premises as the computer data center to the very sophisticated data center that is a copy of the existing system. Depending on the mission-critical operation, the backup facility sizing can determine how much storage a corporation can exercise on a daily basis. The smallest of these companies usually can back up on a daily basis all transactions and date on storage devices as disks cartilages or tapes placing them in a safe storage location. They are used when needed to restore lost information or back up the computer systems if a virus attack takes place, and there is a need to restore lost files. Rebooting and formatting of on-line storage devices take place if viruses are discovered within the system, and thereby bring back and restore all files from the backup systems. Certain information will be not be recovered especially those the ones infected by the virus between storing data and backing up. These types of storage devices are inexpensive and do not require huge financial liability on any corporation, but it is a must to sustain and retain operational capabilities.

The most sophisticated and complex backup system is the totally redundant data center. The Fortune 500 corporations typically have such data centers due to their size of operations and many of them such as banks, health care, and others are mission-critical and have international offices and branches, and operate in many countries around the world. Therefore, they must be always online no matter what, and need to come online through a backup system if and when a cyber attack takes place. Actually, these back up data centers are duplicates of the existing computer centers. Typically, they are located physically in a distant premise. There are dedicated fast network lines especially fiber optic local and lines, and in support for international operation, the use of satellite and other telecommunication mediums will be necessary. Large companies employ different means of fast telecommunication mediums, and many have their own local loop networks such as microwaves and satellites systems to internetwork different locations of their computer systems to backup the facilities data center. In case of any cyber attacks or virus discovery in one of the computer network systems, the online backup facility can be used immediately within minutes to restore operations through directing all transactions to the backup system until the main computer system is rebooted and cleared from any viruses and worms within the main operations. Thereby ensuring coming back online and continuing normal operations.

The cost of setting up a dedicated backup system that is online 24/7 is tremendously expensive, but it is worth the investment if a corporation is a mission- critical operation. In the case of a cyber attack and if the company is considered vitally important to the economy and infrastructure, it is highly recommended to have a dedicated redundant back up facility. The cost might run in the millions of dollars, and dedicated staff are needed to operate both centers therefore bringing the cost even higher, but it is worth the investment in the long run to protect the vital interests and assets of the corporation

e) Cyber Security Auditing

One of the major requirements for companies and organizations to carry out is to do appropriate cyber security auditing on their various computer, networking, and communications systems. This audit will involve not only hardware and software but also people, procedures, protocols, physical security, and other elements of the total operations of the entire computer and network facilities.

Many companies do not understand the importance of such auditing until it is too late, and the cyber hacking damage is done to its' information and facilities. This security audit program must be done by an independent well-experienced security specialist or security auditing companies. There are a number of those companies around the world that specialize in this program. They have the expertise and consultants who are versed in the different forensic audit techniques including cyber attacks with forensic capabilities to not only ensure proper software programs, hardware systems, networking lines, procedures, and protocols, these specialized security audit companies have extensive check listing procedures that can cover every aspect of the requirements and provide thorough auditing to the end users. Any Organization undertaking such audit procedures will be in a better position to discover and realize the weaknesses and vulnerabilities of its' computing environment, and potentially find out if the system has been hacked or any worm or viruses exists. The security auditing program will produce a detailed audit report and a set of recommendations to the CIO/IT managers and top management, to undertake appropriate fixes, upgrades, and cleanups which are needed to bring the system to the level of security status required, and to minimize current and future potential hacking.

Many CIOs/IT managers do not realize the importance of cyber security auditing. The fear of discovering any weaknesses or vulnerabilities in their computing environment will be a liability and might impact their positions with top management. If the audit report to be presented to top management shows these weaknesses, then the manager is considered incompetent and not doing his or her job right. So many managers will not volunteer or suggest to their bosses to undertake such auditing. The cost of auditing is considered high and thereby prohibitive, but necessary, and therefore many IT departments either do not have the budget for it. Many governments and private entities typically have IT departments under the managerial control of the finance department. The IT department is considered a service entity and therefore it is similar to other departments such as HR and other personnel. The IT managers usually have the most difficulties to secure enough budget to keep the computer and network systems operational, let alone asking for extra budget every year for upgrades and on top of this security auditing.

We should not discount the importance of system auditing including security auditing. With the latest cyber attack news coming across from media, the top management will have to realize the importance of computer system auditing. The cost involved in such auditing will be irrelevant to the high cost of loss of valuable data and prestige. The major accounting companies who have to carry out one company auditing per year for companies and corporations, will have, and be based on the request of the top management of the companies, to include system and security auditing in their end of the year financial auditing for their clients. Similarly, government entities who of course do not have to carry out any financial auditing by an external auditing firms, but do have their own government auditing bureaus must include in their auditing practices computer, network, communications, and system security auditing as part of their annual report to top management. The loss of data and information not only for the private sectors but also to government entities is important and critical to protect by any means possible. The cost of spending money on such cyber auditing practices is worth it in the long run. The companies especially in Finance and Health are considered the greatest number to undertake such a security audit, but government entities also who are responsible for the country's infrastructures and security. They should be audited as well. The IT managers must insist on this auditing report every year, and if not granted, they should inform top management how critical it is that without knowing well the weakness and vulnerabilities of the entire systems, protection will be compromised and most likely place the company and entity in danger of operational breakdown and financial losses. They also should and must inform top management in a very clear written statement that without conducting such a security audit, they will not be responsible for future cyber attacks and any potentially liable. This tactic although a bit strong comes from IT managers in many developing countries, and it is highly recommended. Most likely top management would cave in and grant the IT managers their request for the fear that their denial or refusal of such security audit requests would place them in the blaming game and question responsibility. Why not keep such liabilities within the department responsible for the operation of the computer and communication systems department. After all, they are the ones that know well their businesses, and most top managers are not technology driven, lacking the technological knowledge to understand how these systems work. Therefore, IT managers should utilize their technological skills and reinforce their will to on ensure that the systems are operating secure and have all the tools and programs and S/H (software and Hardware) updated and audited regularly.

Chapter Six
Role of CIOs/IT Managers & Cyber Security Experts

The emergence of the different computing and communication technologies from the different classes of computers, routers, storage, and various hardware devices; is combined with the dozens of more of major software systems deployed within an organization, not mentioning the various communication links required and mobile devices that are needed to interconnect the organization's users with the computing environment. This had made the life of the CIO/IT managers unbearable. Furthermore, it is not only software and computing environments in terms of hardware and software they have to worry about, but also the physical and technical security in providing the right access to right individuals. Technical security access means the use of token, user identification, and passwords: while physical security access has to do with accessing building, doors, and restricted areas of a the computing facility. There are many options and technologies to filter through and apply. Recent advancements in physical security access with such biometric authentication technologies and others are now available commercially in the market place. These technologies include fingerprint, facial recognition, hand geometry, retina (eye) recognition, and voice recognition. The most widely used of physical and authentication accesses are: PIN entry key, magnetic cards, and fingerprint recognition. They are the easiest security accesses, and considered more reliable than other technologies. Furthermore, the use of security camera systems have become common in many computing facilities. These security cameras are called CCTV systems or closed-circuit television systems. The most famous of these cameras are the dome-style cameras. They can rotate 180 degrees and can be controlled by an operator attending and monitoring the computer screens.

The changes that occurred to physical security technologies have prompted a dramatic shift to having the computing facility in the back office to now be placed in the front office calling for more strong physical security measures. The complexity of technologies and the requirements in the business and operational world to become more efficient and effective have called on IT managers to utilize whatever technologies are out there on the market that would make a company or entity more competitive, better in serving its clients. The job of the IT/CIO managers has become more demanding. Not only do they have to meet the most advanced and accessible computing technologies, but at the same time provide the means to ensure safety of the computing environment particularly the organization's information and financial assets from cyber attacks and fraud.

The more software applications utilized within organization, the more open and susceptible it is to the computing environment to hacking. It is assumed that for every software system either in terms of technology or applications there are multiple vulnerabilities and loopholes hackers can exploit and penetrate. For example, if Microsoft Windows 7 has at least 50 million lines of codes, it is expected at least 10 percent of flaws within these codes will provide enough vulnerabilities ammunition to any hacker to break in. Therefore, imagine hacking potentially into other software systems, not only operating systems but various other technologies and applications deployed in banking, power grids utilities, public sectors, and a host of services and industries. The more competition we have amongst technology and software companies bringing to the market new applications or updating existing ones, the more vulnerabilities are out there. Software houses are writing as fast as they can, programming and applications codes. They are also using extensive testing methods such as the alpha and beta, but with all these tests the rush to be first in market has created weaknesses in code writing and opportunities for hackers to exploit.

In summary, the Chief Information Officer (CIO), Chief Security Officer, Chief Information Officer or IT managers are all responsible to ensure top management are well informed of all the risks and vulnerabilities of potential cyber attacks. Leadership in this case is most important by these managers to put together a cyber security strategy and to present it to the CEO (Chief Operating Officer) or the board, explaining to them the importance of providing the necessary protection tools and appropriate security methodologies to protect the corporation's most valuable assets which is information. Unfortunately, when it comes to establishing proper security systems for the organization, the IT/CIO mangers are overwhelmed with the computing environment complexity and increasing costs. Thereby, adding another cost which is a cyber security cost which adds another element of higher cost making it prohibitive prompting delays in implementing the cyber security system. It is usually not until a cyber attack hits the facility when the damage is realized, and a lesson is learned, that the company should have allocated all funds required and was asked for by the IT/CIO managers in the first place.

Budget Issues & Cyber Strategy

In order to have a strong cyber security strategy, it requires extensive knowledge by IT managers to understand the implications of not having a proper system patching to fix any vulnerability when a breach to application software is running. IT managers must be able to configure a proper firewall, and to install the right anti-virus software, in addition to other types of cyber protection methods. They do not have to wait until a cyber attack takes place in order to take the matter seriously. Convincing the top management to invest and spend significant sums of money on appropriate securing hardware and software is a major challenge facing many CIOs and IT managers. That is why many corporations have structured their hierarchal organizations whereby CIO and IT positions report directly to the CEO. In developing countries where there is an awareness of cyber threats are even much more lower, and therefore cyber security is the last subject to be concerned about given its high cost. Many CEOs do not realize or understand why they have to spend so much money on computer security systems and back up environments. The only way to understand the importance of cyber security is when their computer networks are hacked and data is lost worth millions of dollars. Of course the blame later is on the shoulders of the CIOs and IT managers who did not put such cyber security strategy forward to top management. It is therefore highly recommended that the IT managers do their due diligence in presenting to top management the worst case scenarios of potential cyber threats to organizations. They also should be mandated to have an appropriate budget and enough qualified personnel to carry out successfully the cyber security strategy.

With the recent internet social media adaptation and latest advancements in technologies for smooth organizational operations, example of financial institutions such banks have embraced them for the purpose of operational times and providing convenience to customers. Becoming competitive in the financial industry has forced many IT managers to utilize the latest computing and internet technologies. With such utilization comes risk of cyber attacks. Therefore, a cyber strategy that can provide protection and can mitigate a cyber attack must be on the top of the agenda of any CIO/IT manager, therefore helping to have a successful operational environment that is less prone to cyber attacks.

It is quite too often that we notice in many companies and in government entities that no one knows what goes on in the organization when it comes to their computer systems and network operations. This is because cyber security information is kept confidential between IT manager and the CEO. Given the fact that CEOs consider IT managers purely technical people operating from back offices and in separate buildings, it is obvious we have broken and limited communications between the two parties. Top managers and their subordinates must constantly be updated and should have proper follow up with and by IT managers to understand their computing environment well. In fact CEOs must have minimum computing knowledge, so they can raise their communication levels in order to communicate well. Different managers at organizational hierarchies must be directly involved in developing the cyber security strategy for the organization. They should understand different specific requirements of software and hardware, in addition to specific applications in meeting different departments' requirements, but not necessarily in detail technical matters yet in overall aspects of business. In understanding cyber danger, top management will be in the position to do their specific operations according to the strategy in place. They would appreciate also the role IT managers play and cooperate closely with in achieving strategy targets. The education process of top managers by IT managers is necessary and must be a continuous process. This education process should cover providing presentations and briefs on the latest computing and technological developments, including potential threats that would come in implementing specific applications and tools that might impact operational and computer networks of that organization. Liability and responsibility of having a successful cyber strategy should be shared amongst all managers within the organization. This would enhance the levels of security needed for their respected entities. Until such cooperation and open communication in a corporate setting has taken place, there will be a huge vacuum with regards to having the IT managers achieve their targeted mission of having to set up the right processes, procedures, and protection mechanism to ensure top level security for the organization against cyber attacks.

The protection of vital infrastructure of a country's computing facilities, make IT managers' responsibilities even become wider and harder. They must have the proper budget to be capable of deploying the best and most advanced of intrusion-detection, firewalls, and anti-viruses in order to protect vital sectors of the country. The budget should not be in this case too limited, otherwise risk of cyber attacks will be so damaging, that countries will face difficulties recovering.

Security Deployment Measures & cyber attack testing

In order to have a secure environment for any corporation against a cyber attacks, it is critical that the deployment of security systems take place. For a small organization, it is important that firewalls in combination of an appropriate backup system be implemented in order to ensure data safety and security, Larger organizations such as multinationals with large numbers of staff, especially those with mission critical operations, deployment of advance and their firewalls, intrusion-detection and anti-virus measures, becomes vital. For having advanced security measures, they can deploy simulation or penetration testing operations. Basically, this process is an imitating hacking attack on the company. Cyber attack testing is actually an attack that is performed on defenses installed within the existing computing facilities. The testing can include sending phishing emails to employees to see how they respond to attached files. It also involves testing hardware systems including servers, routers, network infrastructures, and various computing configurations. This also covers testing the physical side of security, such as site access, and access to restricted areas either computing or networking facilities, staff batches, and doors access grants. These types of hacking testing must be sanctioned and authorized by top management within the executive authority. Testing can be limited and controlled based on agreed upon strategy, as on what to test and what not to test. Such hacking penetration testing is not an easy job to undertake and therefore, certain controls must be exercised, and defined in a detailed agreement between the testers and the organizations to be tested. Some companies will give the testers full power as long as it does not harm existing files and no interruption to ongoing operations that would impact bottom line financial interests of the corporation. The hacking testing job will have a time limit duration from start to end. Detailed reports will be presented to top management showing weaknesses and strengths of the existing computing environment. Suggestions and recommendations on how to improve cyber security will be included in the detailed report. Knowledge of such hacking penetration testing must stay secret and confidential from IT departments and employees working within the corporation. Otherwise, it would defeat the purpose of testing. Only top management and in this case top CEO or COO, and the board will exclusively have such knowledge. Hacking testers would be given written authority in case they are questioned by anyone within the organization. They would be free to proceed without question or any liability. Top management would place one major requirement on the company or individuals doing the hacking testing and that is not to have any kind of testing methods involving tools or kits that would result in having stealth backdoors or worms. If the testers are found to have done such an act, they would be in breach of the signed agreement, and thereby liable.

Hacking penetration testing or simulation of a hacking scenario is considered an important element in the security deployment measures for any critical--mission organization, and for any other corporation that believes in the importance of having such tests to protect its' valuable information, money, and reputation. We have to understand that there is no corporation or organization that is 100 percent secure. They can be compromised regardless of the security measures out in place. However, the level of damage a hacker can achieve either acting on behalf of a nation, individual, or a group of individuals can be mitigated if proper cyber security measures are deployed and upgraded as indicated and illustrated previously.

Cost & Hacking Insurance Policy

The cost of deploying cyber security measures explained earlier is not going to be cheap, but worth the investment in protecting critical information. The additional costs imposed by having cyber security can bring total costs much higher especially when we add additional measures such as protection for company's physical premises. The installation of cameras around the premises, and door access keys with batches for employees which are necessary to ensure that only authorized personal are allowed to access doors and gates are going to be an expensive exercise. These physical protection systems have become indispensable to many corporations to physically protect access to buildings and rooms. Another important step is to make sure all staff working in computing rooms and installations have been vetted and their background is reviewed extensively. There are bad elements out there working within the premises who have necessary accesses and probably fake credentials. They can cause the ultimate cyber threat from inside. Therefore, all staff without exception must have their background checked and examined thoroughly on a frequent basis. We have to understand that cyber attacks do not come only over the internet but can come from within the organization, and especially with people who have access to passwords and backdoor passwords. These people are the computer department's staff we trust in managing company's computing environment. Therefore, the organization must do its' utmost due diligence on its' IT staff reviews and background checks.

With recent cyber attacks reported in the media, many corporations around the world are considering cyber security and cyber attacks as a priority. They now realize that their computing environment is at risk of such cyber attacks, and the subject has become more serious than in the past. CEOs are placing greater pressures on the IT and CIO managers to come up with the right cyber security strategy and action plans.

The on-going and future cyber attacks will not diminish. It is expected to increase in 2015 and years to come given the increase in usage of mobile technologies, and other advanced networking systems. These new technologies have become more and more dependent on the world wide web. New technologies such as cloud computing and mobility have become the new trends in the computing world. This opened the door for hackers and increased the level of hacking. The number of viruses and worms that hackers have found vulnerabilities in, those new technologies are spreading, and starting to take its' toll on many organizations and companies. Companies with enough financial muscle, who are willing to invest in cyber security, and willing to allocate the necessary budget, would be in a better position to utilize the existing tools, kits, and anti- viruses, and firewalls generated by the suppliers of these programs. They are expensive and require huge manpower hours, in addition to hardware and software investment and capital. The smaller firms or companies, who are reluctant to invest now or in the near future in cyber security, will risk cyber attacks. Therefore, it is the responsibility of the IT manager/CIO to bring focus to the potentiality of having these new technologies. They present all potential weaknesses and vulnerabilities in illustrated examples which are understood by the top management especially decision-makers.

The proliferation of hacking through the launch of viruses and worms is going to expand in 2015 and beyond. Various companies and entities in both private and public sectors are going to have to take insurance against hacking and what it will leave behind in terms of financial and data losses. The Insurance companies both in developed and the developing world have enough resources and expertise to deal with cyber security. The will need to employ cyber security consultants and experts. This is going to be a huge challenge given the shortage of such human expertise and the advancement of hacking. Insurance companies will be charged an expensive premium for cyber attacks. This premium cost for many organizations and companies could be prohibitive. The loss to an organization due to cyber attacks can run into millions of dollars. There are recent examples and some of these examples are mentioned in this book such as the Sony cyber attack, where the damage is estimated in the millions of dollars, and not counting the prestige and image of the company. Therefore, many CEOs are considering insurance policy and claims with regards to cyber attacks. Insurance companies are currently planning to include in their organization insurance policies with certain financial claims in cases of cyber attacks. In order to get a cyber attack insurance, the organization will be required to carry out a cyber security auditing program to qualify for having an insurance policy, thereby adding to the total overall cost of having a cyber security strategy.

Wired Countries & Hacking

Developing countries and in particular those GCC countries pride themselves in having their main government departments and companies highly wired to the world wide web. Mobility and computer devices are generously given to staff within these organizations to do their work remotely if needed, which posses main danger and vulnerability for hacking. When we discuss this vulnerability to IT managers and CIOs at major sectors such as banks, Oil and Gas, and government agencies within the GCC countries, we find out that there is less concern of hacking if their computer networks and mobile applications are not going to be impacted by cyber attacks. They believe that due to their firewalls, and intrusion-detection systems, and with the anti-virus programs currently deployed, that they are immune from any attacks. The truth of the matter is attacks are taking place on a daily basis in an alarming numbers. The reports of hacking they receive from the media are only the tip of the iceberg. We all know that 90 percent of hacking incidents are not reported and will not be publicized due to many factors, especially that of loss of reputation. Hackers always have the means under their arsenals of toolkits and little tweet with the source codes to evade and bypass digital signatures of viruses and worms set up by the firewalls, anti-viruses and intrusion-detection systems. This does not mean we should not use existing protection technologies available to us on the market. We need them to provide the minimum protection required. The only difficult part of this scenario with regards to Third World countries including GCC countries, is that there is no stopping those advanced hackers especially those that are state sponsored with financial, technical, and political powers. However, with the Cyber Security road map provided in later chapters, Third World countries can maintain certain cyber security. It must be understood that Third World countries whose protection can embrace recent internet, computing and mobile technologies without having studied closely their impacting on security, will face risks of cyber attacks not only impact them economically but also will threaten their national security.

I remember one banker who holds a senior position at one major local bank in Qatar (a GCC country) while participating in a cyber security seminar at Qatar Foundation (a foundation dedicated to education and health in Qatar and around the world). The seminar was held at Carnegie Mellon University campus which is located within Qatar Foundation. He was telling me that his bank has taken a provision of millions of dollars against potential losses coming out of electronic fraud and hacking. He indicated for example if an ATM or certain accounts were hacked and money was stolen or missing, then bank's provision would cover any losses. He said many insurance companies still do not understand the concept of hacking. However, they do have insurance against standard financial fraud if there were any missing funds. However, due to legal requirements by insurance companies under their insurance claims clauses, the case must be presented to a court of law before insurance companies would be willing to pay for any damages. Hearing this, I wondered what would happen if a number of cyber attacks would increase to the point that such financial bank provision against cyber attacks would not be enough to cover estimated losses. I therefore, strongly believe it is the time for financial institutions within developing countries and particularly GCC countries to take cyber security measures seriously and start investing in appropriate cyber security software and hardware technologies across their organizations and entities.

This is new territory for organizations who are concerned about cyber threats. Insurance companies will need to offer cyber security policies to cover any potential losses, and organizations need to look into this mater and have such cyber security insurance into plans in place policies if provided. Hacking will never stop and we have explained that with the advancement of technologies, hackers will find the means and will be able to penetrate any organization they choose regardless of all cyber security measures out in place. We will hear and see such discussions taking place across countries with regards to having insurance companies providing cyber security insurance policies. This will be a new opportunity for the insurance market to generate business and have a new market to look at.

When I was running a major family business in Qatar, where financial fraud would take place once every couple of years, our legal team needed to come up with enough legal evidence to prove that a fraud had taken place. We took financial provision against financial fraud and there was an insurance policy with a hefty premium. Almost every company must have this. However, given the proliferation of cyber attacks in developing countries, and especially oil rich countries, I know for sure this company and so many others that do not have cyber security insurance policies. In fact, I know for sure that insurance companies in third world countries and in particular GCC countries which are oil and gas rich, do not offer such policies. Similar to financial fraud, insurance companies who are active and pushy when it comes to selling these fraud policies, will pull all the stops out against non-payment to its' clients' claims. The legal teams of a company must work with local authorities in presenting clear evidence and sometimes bring a confession from the culprit in writing to confirm the crime. Only in this case is the insurance company is obliged to pay out, and maybe even not the full amount of fraud damage. Imagine the difficulty of having insurance companies having to pay for a cyber hacking incident claim. First of all, the insurance company must include within the fraud policy, a cyber hacking clause with a fraud insurance general policy. If an insurance company is an advanced one and can produce and sell an independent cyber insurance policy, then we have a major challenge ahead to prove a crime has been committed, and to have any future claims due to nature of the computer hacking. Determining the work of hacking and documenting it legally for local law authorities to understand and judge is not going to be as easy task. This job is not now with company's lawyers as with the classic case of "financial fraud" mentioned earlier, it is now with the IT department. This department which is responsible for providing security to all computing and networking sites and files, and customer accounts, must come up with a definite and highly assured case in order to have the insurance company issuing the cyber security policy, and to convince them and any legal authority with proven evidences which are not easily traced with hackers erasing all of their hacking tracks, to show where and who was responsible for the attack. This situation can be proven if it is shown that the attacks are generated from outside the countries which is very difficult to trace. However, if it is generated within the company or country then the matter becomes easier to investigate and to present legally with the hope that the claims can be collected from insurance companies. I think insurance companies will have difficulty in providing such policies knowing well that the majority of cyber attacks are generated from outside the country and therefore proving and paying for the insurance claims becomes a big challenge to them.

We have noticed in recent times that many of the cyber hacking that has taken place using the open and free wireless networks, or virtual private servers located throughout many countries. For example if a hacker is attempting to target a corporation based in Qatar, the servers where the hacking took place, can be located in another country, and through pivoting from one server to another using a public IP addresses. It would be so hard for an investigator to trace back the source of the attack. Also, some countries who are not willing to cooperate with investigators, would also make it hard to find out the source of the attack especially if these countries are not advanced technologically, which will cause greater delays to locate the hackers, and by the time investigators do find out the real source, the hackers manage to delete any evidence on the server or servers where the attacks are originated from. Regardless, I strongly recommend that any organization concerned with cyber attacks to have such an insurance policy. This will protect the valuable assets, and the proof for law enforcement can be generated and compensation by insurance companies can be sustained.

Chapter Seven
Nations and National Cyber Security

Before we discuss the issue of national cyber security we will need to clarify a few definitions of what we mean. There are many cyber threat definitions. We can break them down into three categories: a) Cyber Wars, b) Cyber Crimes, and c) Cyber Espionage.

a) Cyber War: is basically one country using its' vast technological capabilities in computers and communications systems in attacking another country through sending viruses, or worms. These viruses and worms contain trapdoors and logic bombs. When they are activated they can cause major disruption to economic and financial infrastructures of the targeted countries. In Wars they can disable military command and control centers, and various communications and vital military infrastructures thereby giving cyber attackers superiority in times of wars over other countries.

b) Cyber Crimes: These cyber crimes can take place not only on the net but also it can be an inside job by an individual or a group using computers and information network systems via the internet or through other means such as inserting CD or flash card. Criminal gangs can penetrate a computer system and alter, steal, delete, and modify information and files using various viruses and worms. The objective is purely for financial gain instead of being ideological.

c) Cyber Espionage: When one country or a group of individuals and even one person working solo or with another nation, accesses various computer network and communication systems for the purpose of spying. This would involve listening, copying, altering, and downloading files and various types of information without the knowledge of the intended target being either an individual, a company, or a governmental agency. The objective could be both political and economic in gaining access and stealing vital information that is considered classified. The process does not involve damaging files and data in order not to alert the target being attacked. An attack can continue without the knowledge of the target for a long period of time. Various technologies are used including computers, communication networks, satellites, and mobile listening devices. Attackers use certain programs downloaded from emails sent to the target or by work of an inside job. These files when opened will contain viruses and worms which enable the hacker to carry out necessary espionage activity.

Recent Spy Cases
Kenya

The recent news of police in Kenya raiding a building where 77 Chinese nationals resided made headlines in Africa. According to news reported by officials in Kenya, the Chinese nationals were running a cyber crime network, using sophisticated computer centers with full communications facilities at their residence. The building was described as a house located in an upper class residential area of the Kenyan Capital, Nairobi. The accusation launched by the Kenyan government with the Chinese government was that the 77 member Chinese gang was about to launch a major cyber attack on the nation's communications center. When the raid took place, the police found advanced gears of computers and communication mediums with the intention to cause major damage to financial and communication infrastructures. We do not know how the Kenyan police got the tip and the knowledge of the whereabouts of this gang. The news report mentioned that the finding was by accident due to a fire in a nearby house, and the police had to look into other adjacent houses to clear people. By entering the Chinese house, they discovered the sophisticated gears. The concern by the Kenyan government was in the eventuality of not finding the place by accident and an attack would have taken place. How devastating it would have been on country's infrastructure and ultimately to Kenyan national security. No one can knows if the intention was cyber espionage, as this gangs and others will not leave a trace or evidence for such attacks, and not until the damage is done.

Kenya is bordering other African nations where conflicts and civil wars exist and many tourists are attacked coming from Al-Shabab in Somalia (a Muslim group fighting in Somalia but having terrorist attacks in neighboring Kenya). Kenya is also considered a major tourist attraction, where major revenue comes into the economy. A cyber attack on Kenya's Communication Center would have tremendous economic ramifications on this vital industry. Local newspapers did not mention if there were any previous attacks before the raids and it is expected the government will not reveal such news publically. However, from reading a short article, one would conclude with the size of equipment and gear found at the Chinese gang's home, and the large number of Chinese residing on the premises, that their work had been organized for a longer period of time, and possibly major attacks would have already taken place in the country. As usual Kenyan officials would not report on such attacks for fear downplaying the police and nation security apertures the ability to intercept and secure the borders of cyber threats. However, with Kenya being an open society of high telecommunication network facilities, it is hard to stop such cyber threats especially if the job is carried out by another nation within the border of the country rather than from outside. The Chinese ambassador in Kenya was officially summoned by Kenyan foreign ministry to answer questions and to determine the intention and mission of the gang, and if they belonged to the Chinese government. Good luck to the Kenyan government to get answers from the Chinese government. They will always deny any responsibility, and the answer of course was that these Chinese nationals are acting on their own as an organized crime gang, and the Chinese government has nothing to do with their activities. By the way China is considered a major investor in Kenya's economy and infrastructure, and it has huge political and financial influence, so the matter was closed by the authorities.

Many nations have given great importance to the topic of cyber security. They understood the impact of how cyber attacks can devastate the country's infrastructure. Many nations created Cyber Security Agencies within their governmental echelons. Some countries consider the threat more serious than others by taking military and intelligent approach to the matter. For example, as mentioned before, NATO created a division of Cyber Security, while the United States created both within its' military at the Pentagon, and the same was established by Homeland Security by the National Cyber Security Division (NCSP). Most industrial nations have adapted a similar approach.

While advanced nations look at cyber threats in a more serious manner, a similar approach is looked at from developing countries but with a different approach. Developing countries look at the Cyber threat as a threat that is coming from the Internet, and the use of telecommunication systems. They search for worms and viruses coming via the Internet that might infect personal computers and other technologies which are connected to the net. Therefore, when you ask where their National Cyber Security is located, it is with no surprise, the answer is that it is located within a civilian government agency ether responsible for country's regulation of information system and telecommunications, or a ministry with complete government monopoly on Information and Communications Technology (ICT). These ICTs are government regulatory authorities mandated to set up laws, regulation, standards, training, and to advise other government agencies, and private establishments. This does not mean that Cyber Security Centers in advanced countries do not do basic jobs such as conducting conference, training, producing standards and practices, recommending self-assessment tools, and guidelines. The difference is that advanced nations' centers take legal authority from their military and intelligence agencies in order to enforce cyber security rather than just having to produce recommendations such as other developing nations do.

The Kenyan case and potentially many others in less developing countries can illustrate the importance of intelligence agencies working closely with the government entities. Telecommunication companies operating within the country can provide technological know-how, tools, and assist in ensuring that no cyber hacking takes place within its' borders. Although, the finding in Kenya was by accident, there are many similar potential cyber attacks which have been prevented due to the cooperation of the intelligence agencies of the country with the telecommunication companies. Advanced hacking by nations however is rarely discovered due to the covert operation they undertake.

Therefore, the call for these developing countries to apply legal enforcement authority similar to advanced nations. We can elaborate further in the following chapters when we take GCC countries and in particular Qatar as a case study.

Iran

Iran is one of the Middle Eastern countries who have adapted western technologies from the early modern times of the information age. Subsequently into the revolutionary time, where even with the embargo of all American and some western technologies entering the Iranian market, the country was able to counter this embargo and adapt the latest web and computing technologies out there in the commercial market. In 2009 an active hacker discovered certain weaknesses in Google. This was following an Iranian Google user who was able to bring up the issue, and informed others that there was an a problem with the Google certification. The reason for this news by this hacker is that there was all along a spying process taking place on Google accounts within Iran. Regardless if there were encryption methods used, the hackers managed to intercept secure connections between the browser the Google servers, the attacker managed to decrypt all information coming across, to steal, and spy on all communications going through.

This technique of spying is a standard method used by sophisticated groups and certain nations spying on its' citizens. In the Iranian case, the spying as reported affected thousands of Internet Protocols (IP) addresses, and the finger pointed to the government of Iran spying on its citizens.

Similarly to Google and other internet social media main programs, government with or without knowledge of communication carriers are spying regularly Mobile phone and it is becoming an easy and major target for spying because the device can offer both internet mobility and phone capability. For example, the carrier's IQ program when it is inserted into the root kit of your mobile phone, enables intelligence authorities to track your location, and pass all necessary information logged into the phone to secure sites for spying purposes. The telecom authorities do not inform its users and clients of all inserted programs and there are so many that are produced by nations and companies working with nations to help the intelligence authorities to hack and track targeted citizens without their knowledge. Mobile internet and telephony have become the favored and easiest way of spying on targeted individuals. Hackers and individuals who are trying to avoid and have the knowledge of how the cell or mobile phone work, would not use normal handsets. They would use traditional burn phones which are used for a temporarily purpose and thrown away when calls are completed. These phones are inexpensive and can be purchased from any phone hardware store. They can be filled out with cash in minutes to be used for a certain period of time. These phones are a thrown away and not kept like other expensive phones. These cheap phones have most of the advanced functionalities such as the internet and web search similar to advanced phones. These are the phones used by hackers. In fact, it is so difficult for law enforcement agencies to follow them, because hackers have the ability to turn it back the phone off and disable location activities, and to turn on when the job is required by the hacker.

Developing countries & Mobility Threats

The current advancement in phone technology is astonishing. Current mobile phones are filled with applications and programs that users are not able to do what was not possible five years ago. In fact mobile phones have become the new personal computers, replacing desk tops and other portable devices. However, given the demands by governments law enforcement, telecommunications carriers who are selling these mobile units have filled them with applications and software systems that are considered benign and safe for customers to use or not to use, just being there dormant. If a customer wishes to buy his mobile phone set from outside the telecom carrier domain, then naturally as soon as carrier's sim card is inserted, automatic downloads of these applications and software systems take place, and some of them are seen clearly and others are dormant.

The most useful for law enforcement agencies and similarly to hackers, is the geo-location or GPS program that uses satellite technology to identify the location of a mobile device. Although, some telecom carriers would give the option to customers of using their mobile devices to accept location identification, intelligence agencies and hackers can find out the customer's location easily. Almost all advanced phones have this geo-location with coordinates and within a few feet radius capability. Knowing individual's location has become an important factor in the hacking process. To find out any location, hackers must learn about the individual's habits and travel plans, and here comes the knowledge through social engineering as a means for hackers to build up this knowledge base. In fact, there are software applications that can determine locations based on the pictures and data sharing with others that are connected to the internet, utilizing existing popular social media such as Facebook, Instagram, Twitter, Flicker and others.

Other types of phone connections to be used over the internet is Voice over the Internet Protocol (VoIP). The traditional or office phones that are connected to a large pipeline of either fiber lines and to the server are becoming more common with existing VoIP software applications. People connected via this VoIP can talk cheaply using internet high speed capabilities. For many years since the beginning of this technology, the VoIP was not permitted in third world countries including GCC countries. The reason for that was that the telecommunication carriers monopoly over telephony and any type of networking and communications coming into or out of the country. VoIP would mean less revenue for these government carriers. If an individual is caught using the VoIP system he or she would be persecuted by authorities using laws drawn up to protect a monopolistic environment existing in these countries. Regardless, this VoIP system still until now is considered a threat to revenue and maintaining control over communications by these third world carriers. In fact, if you would like to use this technology on a large scale, and I mean corporate style scale, government carriers would not permit it until you use their hardware and software systems, given the company's legal authority in providing such services even if it is for its' own use. Even commercial stores selling these hardware and software systems must be licensed by telecommunication carriers. These carriers would then sell the necessary bandwidth capacities which are expensive and prohibitive to any company operating within the country. This control stems from the fact that telecom carriers want to maximize their profit from this technology, and to work with intelligence agencies to grant them the ability to monitor and track the activities of a company or individuals connected to this VoIP services.

VoIP can be used by hackers to pivot and relay hacking connection from one server to another, and in multiple locations in many countries. This will make it harder for local and international law enforcement agencies to track and find hackers. If they find any success in tracking, it will take a longer time to locate the source of the attack, and by that time, the hacker has already covered his evidence and moved on. Therefore, Iran and other less developed countries' citizens are becoming aware and realizing how their phones have been used to spy on them, however this awareness is not cascading into their habits of using extensively mobility given the fact that governments' push in having countries that are fully wired. With Edward Snowden's revelations of the United States and other countries spying on its' citizens, many countries realized that all communications carried out over the phone have become a listening post to intelligence agencies. Hackers with the tools and technologies in their hands, have the intelligence and technological capabilities to know that almost all phones have embedded software programs that are intentionally planted by telecom carriers on behalf of the intelligence agencies, without the knowledge of the customer who purchased the phone. Hackers on the other hand, can with different tools in their hands to go around such embedded programs and use different phones and software programs to cover their tracks, still achieving required results over the internet.

The power of VoIP has been realized recently by the hackers, and even commercially by many companies especially those multinational companies that use conference calls and communication medium as an integral part of their business operations. It is now possible to automate VoIP to carry out automatic dialing and even voice messaging to a large number of people in a few seconds and simultaneously, depending on the availability of lines connecting cheaply to the server of VoIP offering almost free calls and messaging systems. With current VOIP software programs in the market today and with a simple engine search systems, hackers can use as many lines as there are available to use for hacking, also to pivot routing to multiple carriers and providers. These software programs that are available commercially in the market have the technological intelligence to provide hackers an ability to scan a range of phone numbers, analyze audio, and determine the type of system used from the other end of the call either it is a voicemail, a modem or a computer system. All these technologies and tools are available to hackers given current and future advancements in mobile technology. It has become an easier task for any hacker to identify targets in terms of their behavior and also their location and addresses. All of this information collected would also enable the hacker to work on setting up the foundation to have an easier means to launch the attack.

Access to information throughout developing countries and in particular GCC countries has become easier than in the past due to widespread use of internet websites by almost every company and governmental organization. If you do not have a website and it has to be comprehensive and technology loaded to support mobility and various social media, then the company or government agency is not up to date with the new age of technology and therefore would be considered outdated. Here comes the ability of hackers to obtain basic information and in many ways even detailed background on the target organization and its' staff through the process of reconnaissance. This function is the first major function of any successful hacking. Those reconnaissance activities include searching websites of the targeted companies and collecting information on target's technology used in its' computing environment. Company websites could be a major source of information about a company's infrastructure and its' employees. It is not necessary to have technical information, however, the non-technical information such as press releases and news media are as important. They are mainly reported on the company's website, an can be a great source of information on existing and future computing plans within the company. The existing internet search engines available to us today, enables hackers to collect not only the non-technical information which is generally available on company websites or any associate websites, but also technical information where hackers can use tools and code writing ability to search for company use of any anti-viruses malware, remote capabilities, mail and webmail system uses, and any IP addresses used by the company. Furthermore, many of the IT companies around the world provide press releases of their success in launching and successfully implementing computing programs and applications in many organizations and corporations. These types of press releases are considered valuable to hackers where they can dig deep into such information, and obtain so much insight in the technological and computing infrastructure put in place. It is so strange even within those less developed countries that defense and military intelligence news are available on websites of many software companies who carried out implementation for these organizations and entities.

Another weakness in these less developed countries where hackers have been so successful through mobility is use of spearhead phishing. Email systems are currently used more and more through the mobile phones by individuals and company's employees who are on the move and need to be in communication constantly. Remote access to email systems using mobility have become widespread within many of less developed countries. Phishing websites are commonly used by hackers in copying an existing website and routing the targeted person thinking that he or she is accessing the real website. Hackers have tools at their disposal to copy and clone a website. These tools are automatic, enabling hackers to copy, and once the hacker get its' hand on the source code of the login page and to copy it to a file. Hackers must be familiar with programming scripts such as Java in script files and changing source codes. This will generate a website page to enter the necessary required information that is so useful to launch any required cyber attack. Target users when entering the identification name and typically passwords, will receive a message indicating to them wrong and incorrect, and to try to reinter again, thereby keeping records of all necessarily passwords on company employees. Furthermore, hackers need to have also an elaborate scheme to ensure no suspicious activities are generated when a user of a website logged is in. Hackers are able to copy the site down to the font used, so the look and feel is the same, also to register the domain name of the website. This will not be same name but a variant of the original name, and this will look like the same name with a letter or a number change that is not noticeable by the target accessing the cloned website. When the target user is redirected to the copied website page, it is so easy to redirect the target to the malware page that will be able when accessed to deploy the hacking worm and virus. All this is done with simple code writing and scripting using available commercial languages such as Java scripting and other script languages. Hackers even without having the technical capabilities of writing sophisticated scripting to spearhead phishing, can obtain these tools from commercially available hackers' websites. There are many internet engine search, books, and tools that are available worldwide which hackers can have easy access to. Furthermore, hackers with sophisticated tools and programming abilities can use rogue hardware to access points which can intercept all traffic generating from a target user's laptop or mobile unit connected to a server or a default gateway. The way this type of hacking is carried out, is by routing the target individual to the hacker's open wireless network, and by sending to the target user a denial of service attack. The target user as a natural response will try to use any open wireless network to connect, which is the hook for a hacker and the prey is now connected to hacker's network rather than the original one whereby a server is programmed to gather all credentials and any communications carried out by the target accessing the website.

Spearhead phishing which is commonly used across the GCC countries which can be done either as mentioned earlier using the internet and wireless networks or by any storage devices internally depending on the specific target. These devices are the trojans that would carry worms and viruses used by hackers. It is always assumed that the Stuxnet attack on the Iranian nuclear plant was carried out by a Trojan device, most likely a an inserted CD or USB drive or a stick. The cyber attacker would resort to internal types of attack because of the difficulties of accessing targets using the internet and any wireless network system. Depending on the attackers' sophistication and who is behind them, internal uses of storage devices carrying programs containing worm or virus are done in a stealth manner, which means the target will not notice their computing systems have been infected and compromised. This action is typically carried out by intelligence agencies in maintaining maximum secrecy of their attacks. But, if such stealth environment is not provided for by the virus or worm, then it is easier for investigator to trace back the attack to the source. In the case of the Iranian nuclear facility it is believed that the officials who were implicated in participating in an inside job in having used storage devices to launch the Stuxnet virus have been identified and punished, however, I am sure there is more to this story that what we learned so far.

With the advancement of the mobile devices be it a mobile phone, iPod, laptop, or any mobile device that can be connected to any personal computer that is connected to the main server, the hacker has always has an advantage of having insider knowledge in doing what he is commissioned to do. These devices have huge storage capacities that can carry huge files containing all types of viruses and worms. For example, the simplest phone nowadays can have over 512 RAM processor, more than 4 megapixel camera, over multiple gigabytes of internal storage and a huge size of gigabytes exceeding the 32-gigabyte with SD card the size even gets bigger, a wifi interface that would easily connect the user to any public or private wireless network, and many other features such as data mobility and connection. In fact, these mobile device can be used as a delivery mechanism for hackers' worms and viruses. With intelligence agencies' abilities to tap into any devices even including mobile phones around the world and establish a root within the phone to act as if it is the hacker's phone, the attacker can launch a virus whenever it is connected to a website or company server, and this is also the case with other mobile devices. The more sophisticated the mobile device, the easier for intelligent authorities to access it. This is due to many applications and software systems that are filled with vulnerabilities and in which hackers can exploit. Not only do hackers use such mobile devices to launch viruses and worms but also it is a spying tool to listening to phone conversations, read and monitor emails, view pictures and videos, and have location identification, and do practically whatever the mobile can do without having the owners know what is going on. In fact, a hacker can even turn on and off the phone if required. It is so surprising that many mobile devices are coming preloaded with applications and software programs. This is to make it easier for the average and non-technical users to start using them without the hassle of getting into the technical jargons of installing or knowing them. They can just use them as they come. The danger here is that these mobile devices when they are purchased or gifted, are preloaded with worms and viruses and the only way to use the device is to wipe them clean from any pre-installed programs or apps using the formatting command, and re-install them with the use of the anti-viruses and other tools that can discover the potentiality of having root hacking programs.

Therefore, there is real danger for developing countries and mainly GCC countries, where many expatriate community's work in the IT sector, and especially in government establishments and vital sectors of countries' infrastructures. We can assume that given one disloyal and disgruntled foreign employee might insert the USB stick or CD drive into his personal computer that is connected to where he works, and to launch a virus or a worm into the computing network of the entity. This is how easy it is for a cyber hacker to accomplish the job and cause intended damage. Intelligence agencies as mentioned do not even have to recruit spy or inside hacker, they can and will use available technologies and tools in their arsenal to launch an attack. For these less developed countries, the problem is with certain individuals and groups that are intended to cause harm to infrastructures for political reasoning or any other agenda. The danger is coming from within. The intelligence agencies which have to do their work in a stealth environment and make it extremely difficult for developing countries' entities to discover that hacking and spying is in progress and continuous. Many organizations have become aware of the danger in allowing any external storage device to be plugged into their computing networks. However, due to the lethal approach of directly inserting a virus or worm into a computer facility instead of going through the hassle of wireless or remote login where success rates might be low, has become the easiest approach for hackers. Chances of stopping the use of such external storage and delivery devices into any organization is an impossible task to achieve, as they are becoming smaller and smaller in size and have high storage and memory capabilities. They can be so tiny and small that an insider can insert them into the USP pin and launch a Trojan worm installed within it and it will automatically work without any additional programming required. Therefore, less developed countries and in particular the GCC countries will witness more cyber attacks from inside jobs. The continuation of hacking threats will remain and will actually increase in the coming months and years.

Chapter Eight
Software Companies: Oracle & SAP

There are many software companies in the world and the majority are located in western world which have introduced and still bring up into the market some of the most powerful technologies impacting our daily life and business world. There are many computer and technology giants in the market today, however for sake of focus and understanding who are the main players in the software business world, and which company has the power to impact software and hardware cyber security, two companies come into the picture. Our focus will be on two major software company giants. They both between them command a strong market share in software technology and applications. One is an American from the Bay area of San Francisco, in the United States, and the other is a German company. Both companies dominate the software world and between them have almost a 90 percent hold on the major Fortune 500 companies, and a large percentage of medium and large companies around the globe. They are massive in terms of capital and personnel. They have offices in almost every country in the world. So many companies cannot operate without their automation. They are Oracle and SAP.

Oracle came from the business world where its' relational data base created the first powerful search in an innovative way, and is the first of its kind. Oracle developed early on, this relational database engine for the US military. This new database use relationships amongst a number of identified fields to specifically locate and in a quick manner request data. Prior to this technology, the computing industry only knew sequential searches of data. This means the search has to be carried out in a sequential manner throughout a file until specific data is found. Search time and speed has made all the difference between the two types of searches. This distinguishes Oracle from the rest of other companies and provides a competitive edge over others. It was the start of rising star in the software industry.

Just imagine a stored file where there are millions and trillions of data stored in different fields. In comparison to older data bases that are sequential, it would have taken the computer with its' powerful speed much longer time to search and find the requested data. The Oracle relational database was revolutionary. The success of this relationship data base made Oracle what it is now, a leader in this business and managed to build on such success and embarked on different platforms of software technologies and applications in supporting the business environment. The ERP (Enterprise Relationship Product) was then launched and became a major success. It became the industry standard, and a major seller in its arsenal of the so many products listed.

While SAP was created by four employees from IBM who left the company and started their own company based in Germany. Its' beginning was to design a software engineering product that would help control automation in the major industrial companies, the beginning of the first industrial automated control products. This is followed by its' own ERP similar in its' functionality of Oracle following the increasing demands by industrial clients. This was followed by so many products that are in serious competition to the Oracle. Now, the two companies are competing with each other. They are dominating the software market share for not only for the large Fortune 500, but also for medium and large enterprises both in the business and government worlds. SAP is so familiar and most famous in industrial companies, while Oracle has dominated financial and public sectors. Both are now competing in almost every market. If you approached either company, you would get a long list of products similar in functionalities but with different terminologies and technological jargon names. The two companies have greatly contributed to advancements in information systems' technologies through their research and development efforts. They have been able to recruit highly intelligent people to develop software applications thereby advancing business efficiency and productivity. They also in the past 10 years and through their massive cash liquidity acquired many smaller companies offering either complementing products or products that would enhance functionalities of their existing list of commercial products to be sold all over the world. If you look at their websites and search for their product listing, one would be amazed how many there are, covering every aspect of the business and operational world. There is almost something for any need or requirement, and if it is not on the list, then the team of consultants and project management staff are ready for any task required. They can develop and write the right programs and modify software applications to meet their clients' requirements. I remember when I was heading one of the largest family businesses in Qatar, there was a requirement to have an auto dealership software application which both companies did not offer many years back. They would rely on third party programming houses to do the job. The family business was in the auto retail business, and needed this software application to manage various business activities from sales, rental, service, parts, and many others. Oracle was responsible for the delivery of the product, and when the third party which was an Oracle partner failed to deliver the product, Oracle stepped in and took charge of it, and had its consultants finish the development phase in record time in order for it to become operational.

These two large software powerhouses have been major contributors to current and future productivity and efficiency of many major governments and business enterprises around the world.

Oracle & SAP Cyber Security Approach

The two companies have launched many products related to security thereby complementing clients' requirements of data and access. They would gladly offer security tools and technologies to their clients especially when selling their data bases and various applications. Oracle in particular have been supplying access verifications, and data protection. It supplies data encryption software to the Department of Defense (DoD) in many countries. It would be surprising to know with having such high security tools and technologies on DoDs' main computers that are supplied for example by Oracle, many of DoDs' and in many countries, do not have proper anti-virus programs thereby making them susceptible to attacks by hackers. They can use existing vulnerabilities in many desktop operating systems and applications, and therefore use them as gateways into main computer facilities.

When it comes to Oracle and SAP software systems, they are typically run on a different operating systems than desktop personal computers which are basically Microsoft Windows, or Apple operating systems. The Oracle and SAP software technologies and applications are run on higher level operating systems such as Unix and Linux. They have different programming languages than PCs, and therefore offer different challenges to hackers. Unfortunately, nothing is impossible to intelligent hackers who are willing to learn and master these programming languages and write codes containing a worm or a virus. One of the languages used in writing operating codes is SQL (Sequential Language). Hackers have managed to insert their codes into the SQL codes running different software technologies and applications developed by the two software companies, i.e. Oracle and SAP. This technique of code writing into SQL is called SQL-injection.

The matter of cyber threats has been addressed constantly by two software companies when and attending to its' clients' fear and security requirements. They always will provide assurances of offering the best products in protecting stored data and eliminating unauthorized access to network facilities. They can offer certain levels of comfort in offering the different software technologies and security applications, but then they will not be able to ascertain total security to clients. Given the fact that cyber attacks can be generated from internal source either by a rogue individual or a group of people intended to insert the coded virus or worm internally, and have access to the administration system, or have the access authority level to modify and update, it is very difficult to maintain a 100% secure system.

In any computing facilities where there are multiple jobs running the show, two of the most important and sensitive positions are Data Base Administrators (DBA) and Network Managers (NM). They know every element of computing technology, applications, and networking communication. These people have the ultimate power in having complete access authority at the highest levels. They have custody of backdoor accesses and passwords, and all related computer operating systems and administration . It is important for top management to have these two positions always on a watch list, especially in the case of cyber attacks. They will have to answer to top management as to how a cyber attack took place and what damage was done to organization's operations.

Three main themes are offered by the two software giants, Oracle and SAP, in selling their security tools. They will offer to clients full security suits of products involving Data Security, Identity Assurance, and Access Management. Additionally, they also offer tools providing authentication and authorization requests for accessing any data. To top it all an encryption can be added to the list of tools, thereby comforting customers when it comes to data security. This security mechanism can be provided for online operations and for storing data on tapes or desk drives as backup. It is believed that even if the hackers manage to steal and download any data, and if such data is encrypted, then it would be useless data, and the only way to understand it is to decrypt it. This is not the fact anymore. Decryption has become a non-issue with many advance hackers especially the ones working for spy agencies around the world. Companies coming from countries who are selling such encryption tools already have decrypted tools made available to spy agencies through legal governmental requirements, and if not then such advanced spy agencies would have all technological means to decrypt. One would think that the information downloaded DoD files by Bradley from USA (a rogue military personal) to WickiLeak, was encrypted. Think again. Oracle claims that USA DoD is one of its' biggest clients, and if we assume that their data bases are not Oracle-based, then can we assume that downloaded DoDs' files and videos were not encrypted. This assertion would have been highly questionable. Many DoDs around the world would go to great lengths in encrypting highly sensitive files, and in the case of the USA DoD, these downloaded files contain highly sensitive materials with regards to the United States involvement in two wars, in Iraq and Afghanistan.

If we take Oracle, which has the most technologies and applications running in any business and government environment, one will notice that their best selling products and foundation for early success are enterprise applications supported by Oracle technologies,. These products manage day to day operations of businesses and governments. Applications can range from basic salary, human resources, inventory, recruitment, procurement, sales and marketing, distribution and supply chain management; to more highly sophisticated applications such as plant operation and online transactions. On top of all these enterprise products, they can also offer system and process auditing. Such auditing ability is offered through their highly structured guidelines and processes to produce lists of specific strengths and weaknesses, enabling the clients to understand where are the areas that needed more attention and in case cyber security. Currently, technology has advanced to discover any cyber attack existing. Oracle and other competing companies offer companies automatic tools in having system auditing. This automatic auditing is critical for forensic staff to discover discrepancy transactions. It can also offer transactions log comparison. This is an important step in finding out if there is a cyber attack.

The list of applications are so extensive and can run in multiple pages. It is called the bill of materials similar to the inventory bill of materials. The main money making machines are not in selling these applications which of course can bring in certain levels of revenue, but in selling the technologies behind them. At the heart of these technologies is the data base administration. This is further supported by other technologies such as middleware, mobility and many new ones that are sold in stacks to customers around the globe. All of these technologies are of course updated and upgraded constantly, and with license fees to be paid upon using them, and they are yearly licenses, in which software companies can maximize their profit margins.

SAP started a different path from the beginning, but then became in the same sphere as Oracle. SAP started in selling Industrial Specific Applications focused on running major industrial platforms. Its' beginning was in Germany, supplying and managing automotive and various other industrial companies, and spread across Europe. Now SAP offers the same bill of materials of software technologies and applications, it hardly can be differentiated from Oracle except in terminologies. Both companies aggressively compete head to head against each other for the same market share in each country around the globe.

Oracle and SAP are now promoting their new technologies which is mobility, which is spreading fast within not only in the private sector companies but also in governments' entities. with governments in the Gulf Countries, namely the six GCC countries, including Qatar which has one of the highest internet and mobility penetration amongst developing nations. The risk of cyber attacks therefore becomes much more urgent to address. There is no security solution to this rise of mobility and internet connection where mobile devices not only highly intelligent phone units, but also iPads and other mobile devices that are basically not just only acting as basic phone but personal computers on the move. Currently, few applications offer necessary anti-viruses on these mobile devices, but unfortunately, many of them do not have them, thereby making them open to hacking. Acquiring required sensitive passwords and other confidential information has become easier for hackers . All types of confidential information are stored on these devices either by accident or intentionally by not realizing that it is a matter of time for a hacker to find his way as explained in previous chapters to access such information. The mobile devices are linked on-line and in frequent rates to the main computing environment, and therefore there is the difficulty for companies such as Oracle and SAP to protect main software technologies and applications residing on main systems from hacking. However, the two companies are working in assuring that such mobility links can be managed in terms of access security, however such efforts are not working against advance hackers, and we constantly hear news of cyber attacks on major private and government establishments around the world. Oracle and SAP have paid attention to this factor when approaching government entities and trying to promote implementation of cyber security applications on mobility and data protection on the computer systems of the public sector entities. Unfortunately, this comes with additional costs, and many decision makers in deciding budget requirements especially for the IT department, feel that such high security of its' data is not necessary and thus opening doors for cyber attacks. Oracle and SAP also started offering security applications not only to industrial companies given their software complexity in handling large industrial complexes, but also to DoDs and other public sector entities with tools of access, authorization, identity, and encryption management tools. However, when a cyber attack takes place either at the industrial complex or government entity, then the essentiality of data security became obvious to the client. That is when one of the two software houses are called in by clients to discuss what happened and how to protect its data and network system going forward. If it is found that this entity lacks proper security tools, both companies would recommend appropriate cyber security tools and technologies to maximize data and access protection.

No one knows the amount of the cost of cyber attacks on the GCC six countries. Unfortunately, the data is not available either from private or public sectors in how much millions or billions of dollars are lost to cyber attacks within these countries. The authorities either at the government ICT level or general statistic departments have not produced any reports on the magnitude of the amount lost to cyber attacks. We will need more research into this matter, and until such research is published, we will not know the extent of such damage, and to have the authorities of both sectors aware of associated risks with cyber attacks on the national economy of the country. The two software powerhouses (Oracle & SAP) have the responsibility being in the field in supplying the required software technologies and applications to these countries, and almost have a monopoly on the decimation of information and communication technologies to countries, that they have the responsibility to collect and publish reports and studies on cyber security issues for the GCC countries and per country illustrating different risks associated with cyber attacks, and total financial losses. Additionally, certain statistics are required to understand what are the percentages of attacks and where they are coming from? For example, we will need to know what percentage is coming from an external source or internal; if hacking is done over the internet and electronically by launching viruses and worms; or by physical attacks through intentional damage to existing hardware and networking facilities. This will be helpful to raise awareness amongst decision makers and public officials across the six countries.

Although, the two software giants have commercial purpose in mind and practically do whatever the clients ask for in terms of cyber security, the public sector in particular puts all its faith in government agencies which is the ICT (Information & Communications Technology), which is the highest authority in charge of providing and protecting the public sector information and communication systems. In working with ICTs of the GCC countries, for Oracle or SAP has not been an easy path. Understandably, ICTs would like to monopolize and control dissemination of computing and networking technologies across government entities, and to promote new technologies and applications such as mobility and the internet. While Oracle and SAP would like to work in having decentralized environment knowing well that each government entity has its own unique requirements that cannot and will not be fulfilled by the ICT being a central authority. I am in total agreement with the philosophy and approach toward working closely with government clients. Oracle and SAP must work closely with central government authorities in meeting their specific requirements, and understand potentiality and risk associated to data and infrastructures especially when it comes to the matter of cyber attacks. Protection of country's national and vital infrastructures, and in providing maximum national security protection against any cyber attacks within and outside the borders should be a shared responsibility between these two big commercial companies and governmental agencies.

Oracle and SAP Bills of Materials

The common complaint by clients using the two software houses is that they offer so many products in their list of products (bill of materials). The challenge for companies' staff is in matching customer requirements with products listed in the Bill of Materials. These products are listed and published over the internet at each company's websites, and descriptions and further details are also available. Both companies have consultants and expertise to discuss, analyze and present right solutions to clients in meeting existing and future requirements. The main cyber security software technologies and applications offered by the two companies are summarized around the following:

a) Identity & Access Management: The concept here is to ensure that any person granting access to the computer network system of an entity is the right person. These tools or applications associated with technologies offered by the two companies provides controls on access and identifying processes. Unique user identification and unique passwords are used. The tools require the person wanting to access the system to provide additional identification information on top of user id and password. This is just to add more security elements to controlling access. The "single sign-on" is considered one of the greatest selling points by the software houses to secure access by any employee or outside authorized person to the company's computing environment. There are multiple layers of access and user identification depending on sensitivity of the computing site. In many say DoDs and intelligence agencies, the user who would like to connect to a computing environment is not only asked to input their User Identification and Passwords as a first level, but then the user is present with another screen to enter further identification information only he or she knows and entered before as authorized user, this second and probably third level, will provide maximum identification controls required by any security conscious organizations.

Then we have access management tools that would control if this person who logged in and already passed the identification process, and allowed them to enter into the computing environment of the entity, which must have certain access rights and controls as to what type of applications and data to see, retrieve, print, and other functionalities. The level of access to certain data is preprogrammed through the access management tool. It enables system and data base administrators to generate a table of access controls as to who and at what level of data access can be provided to any particular application and specific file.

The identity and access managements solutions are considered the first front door protection against cyber attacks, and they are highly recommended by the two companies dealing with private and government entities within third world countries and in particular the GCC market. They are highly recommended to public sector organizations as they host most vital information on public sectors and its' citizens as health and education.

b) Database Security: Databases are considered the most vital aspect of any computing environment. There within these databases where organization's full information is stored. The two software giant's basic selling point to any new organization is to offer their database technologies and tools to administer it. Knowing well that by moving from manual to automated environment requires that entire records and information stored on papers now is in an electronic database where they can be accessed and retrieved on a single stroke from keyboards of computer devises. Hackers usually know that by accessing the database, an access to vital information is then possible. Of course the first level of hacking is to go through identity and access controls, and then with having that ability and knowing they are already in the system, it is easy to download the data, manipulate or destroy it from the database. Thus, the requirement to provide an additional security to such vital databases has become inevitable and essential.

In order to protect databases, the solution provided by the software houses, is that access to what type of files and data stored is controlled on a transaction level. Only authorized personal can access certain files and records, and this follows with authorizing controls at transactional levels. This will can provide additional security protection levels.

Furthermore, databases and all of its' contents can be encrypted and only people with appropriate keys which are considered highly confidential, can view information stored in the databases. It is well-known that many of highly security conscious organizations are employing encryption solutions and incorporating them in access solutions. So, if a user is identified and would like to access certain files and require certain transactions, he or she would be required to use his encryption key which is basically a sequence of numbers and letters generated to accommodate decryption of transaction information. This ensures not only that viewing the data is confidential and it is impossible for hackers to recognize transactions as it will look gibberish to them, unless they have in also access to the decryption key. Only advanced and sophisticated hackers belonging to sophisticated spy agencies, with technical abilities of decryption.

Cyber attacks might happen when data is shared between one public organization or others. For example, there are always major requirements by many agencies, specifically public sector organizations to send and share information amongst themselves, the online transactions of transmitting files and records over online and the internet thereby become an open field for hackers to intercept the transmission and have access to confidential information. The only recommendations in this case is to provide hard wired access through certain communication links that would go around the internet connection. Although, these direct hard wired links do not of course provide total security, but with database encryption and other solutions and access administration systems provided by the two companies, Oracle and SAP, the public entity can minimize security threats coming from hackers.

That is why in this database security environment that the database administrator, called DBA for short, who have direct and privilege access to all types of transactional records at every level within the database, is a highly important person within the computing environment of any organization. This person maintains high technical skills and is usually highly paid, and must undergo extensive security checks, and verified clearance before they get this job. Such skills are not available amongst the wider local nationals of each of the member countries of the GCC countries. The majority of staff work as DBAs in the GCC country are of expatriate nationalities coming from different countries. They work in sensitive government agencies including the department of defense and certain intelligence agencies. Unfortunately, the authorities of these GCC countries do not realize how important this DBA function is in maintaining maximum security for vital information and protection against cyber attacks.

The Oracle security products are:
a) Oracle Identity Management which contains solutions such as Identity Administration and Governance, Access management, and Directory Services.

b) The Database Security Solutions would include: Oracle Advanced Security and Oracle Database Vault (this solution provides limitations of power of privilege users and enforcement of segregation of duties), Oracle Database Audit Vault (security all data into one secure repository), Oracle Data Masking (having multiple database platforms), Oracle Database Firewall (first line of defense where monitoring of database activities and the prevention of SQL-injections attacks), and finally Oracle Label Security (multi-level data access control based on data classification on a "need to know basis").

The SAP Security Product List are:
(a) SAP Enterprises Threat Detection (maintaining log data on application, database and operating system).

(b) SAP Event Stream Processor (combined with SAP HANA platform analysis and logging of all transactional data)
With the above two main cyber security solutions the organization can maintain a log on all the transactional activities. This can be analyzed for unauthorized access and to what level of data, and also provide an automatic alert for any incoming unauthorized access on multiple levels. Access and identity alert can be provided to most sophisticated transactional levels. It also alerts those unauthorized users access to certain levels of data. The SAP Enterprise Threat Detection for example can be customized to include and incorporate any potential detection for threats and the production of logs to investigators. This is all done in a real time monitoring environment and can be carried out in an ad hoc analysis of existing and potential attacks.

I believe the two companies (Oracle and SAP) control over 60 percent of the software landscape of the companies and public entities in the GCC six countries including Qatar. They have the ability to provide certain levels of cyber protection requirements through their security solutions and tools. They of course, do not guarantee a fully secure environment. We should not discount other major software and hardware suppliers such as Microsoft and IBM. They are also very active in the GCC market and both have targeted small, medium and large organizations. We know for sure that IBM has been in GCC market for over 30 years and have their major hardware and software installed and operated by many government entities such as the military. However, the two software giants Oracle and SAP were able to penetrate the market more strongly especially with medium and large enterprises and establish their footprint across the region.

Interconnection with internet and the utilization of different mobility devices ranging from smart phones, tables, and mobile PCs have been overwhelming. Many large computing companies including Oracle and SAP have launched cloud solutions to take advantage of such mobility interconnections to the internet. Due to such increasing mobility and interconnection, and the use of cloud computing, we will witness more risks associated with cyber attacks, and this will be coming in a higher rates in months and years to come. Therefore, the largest software companies have the obligation and probably the commercial incentives to offer better and more improved security solutions to handle the increasing emergence of mobility, with high interconnection with the internet. I am certain we will see these security solutions come into the market in coming years. As the awareness of the danger and potential damage from cyber attackers increase, there will be more pressure on these software companies to fulfill demands and the requirements of cyber security, being consumer-centric which is the key for their success in maintaining market share and expanding it.

It is imperative for the big software companies to contribute to cyber security awareness and education of the GCC countries. There are no excellence centers or training facilities within GCC countries on cyber security. Contribution to educational and awareness efforts of the society and country they are operating in and making millions of dollars in sales and profit every year, should be part of their community services. In fact, current training centers are purely commercial ones and generate income to all the software companies operating in the region. There has to be a change of policy and direction with regards to community service. They have to give back to the community.

I suggest that a certain percentage of their income be dedicated to such free education and training to be established in the GCC market, and not by regulatory enforcement but by self interest of maintaining good community governance and good contributions to society. The educational awareness of cyber threats given the wide spread phenomenon of hacking and in an era of mobility where GCC countries are considered the highest users of mobility in the Middle East. This is an important task to be undertaken by these software companies.

One program I do remember that the two companies Oracle and SAP got involved with, is an internship training program for local university graduates. The program is managed from an educational training facility for Oracle and SAP outside the GCC countries. This program basically shows that these companies are interested in educating local nationals who would like to have an internship program for one year whereby these new trainees can then join the work team of the two companies, if they are qualified and turn out to be good. Unfortunately, these efforts did not go smoothly in a number of countries within the GCC. The fact that GCC countries are considered amongst the richest in the Middle East, and the fact that local nationals are still a small population and considered the minority compared to the huge expatriate and laboring force working there. It therefore, was an unsuccessful program in many countries within the GCC. Large multinational software companies are not committed socially or by any government regulations to spend on social programs. Setting up free training programs, or even having free workshops will definitely raise awareness and educate the general population especially the local nationals of the importance of cyber threats and hacking. I am sure such efforts will be happening soon, and local authorities from ICTs across the GCC will play a major part in cooperation with these software companies to spend more on social programs. We cannot deny that these companies are active in promoting such social programs in less developed countries either in Africa or Asia, but the time has come to do the same for the GCC countries.

Chapter Nine
GCC and Cyber Security

In order to understand the cyber security capabilities of the six gulf countries namely: Saudi Arabia, Kuwait, Qatar, Oman, Bahrain, and United Arab Emirates: we will look at one country in particular and focus on it as a window into the other countries. Why we are doing this? Because all these countries are joined together as one political, economical, social, cultural, sport, and all other sectors as one entity. They have common heritage and culture, and speak the same Arabic language with similar accents. They are close in geographical proximity to each other, and in fact if you travel by air from one country to another it is less than one hour.

Qatar for example, like its' sister GCC countries, is ranked 23rd out of 148 countries in Networked Readiness Index. This Index is regularly given by the World Economic Forum 2014. Qatar is the most wired amongst many advanced wired nations, and just recently rolled out country's wide broadband fiber optic link under the National Broadband Plan in place. The country witnessed massive growth in the economic sense since discovering and exporting gas to the world, in addition to its' current oil production which is not as massive as its' neighboring countries such as Saudi Arabia and Kuwait. Due to Oil & Gas revenue, the information and communication technologies the (ICT) market witnessed an increase at the rate of 7-10 percent depending on the most independent reports coming out from major consulting firms such as Booz & Company. ICT market size in total sales reached approximately 25 billion dollars in 2016, and it is expected to grow more as major sporting events are taking place in coming years and in particular the World Soccer Cup in 2022. To be high on the interconnectivity index level being a top country amongst developing countries is commendable and the people responsible for such advancement of internet connectivity and mobility must be accredited. It is also important to realize with such high interconnectivity and mobility as a wired country to the world, the rate of cyber attacks is going to increase in multiple numbers, and therefore will increase level threats to vital infrastructures and national security.

The GCC countries enacted different types of laws such as the Critical Information Infrastructure Protection Laws. These laws which are approved by the cabinets of each country, provide guidelines for the protecting of key infrastructures mainly power grids, oil and gas production, financial transactions, healthcare, and government operations. Additionally, each GCC country introduced a New Cyber Security Law offering better protection to individuals and businesses. At the same token while the two laws given certain comfort to the country's protection against cyber threats, each country has launched Qatar's e-Gov program to provides user-friendly access using mobile devices from anywhere into different government websites offering electronic services to its citizens and residents. These e-Government strategies are master plans to ensure high numbers of on-line government services to all, reaching 100 percent in the coming 10-20 years. Furthermore, each country had to move into more improved versions of the unlimited IP addresses from the existing and limited IPv4 platform and into the IPv6 protocol which will enable the IP address to accommodate from a 32 bit to 128 bit address which means more addresses can be allocated as the demand for IP addresses increases.

I know much about these countries technological advances especially in the area of Information Systems and Telecommunications. I have written my doctorate thesis on the GCC Information Systems and Telecommunications. I was one of the first gulf citizens from State of Qatar to be deployed in serving my country upon my graduation to the headquarters of the GCC in Riyadh, Saudi Arabia. I spent 8 years managing two departments at Economic Affairs. The departments are responsible for the promotion of joint regulatory, policies, and procedures with regards to IT, and Telecommunications for the six nations. The position was coordinating and having the six countries agree on regulations and policies, and to push them for implementation. The process was done through the various committees set up by the headquarters, similar to the European Union, where regular meetings would take place to introduce new guidelines or policies, and to follow up on the agreed up recommendations.

When it comes to the subject of information systems and telecommunication technologies in the 1980s, the six nations were in their infancy with regards to cyber threats. In fact, I do not remember that we have ever discussed the seriousness of such threats on the infrastructures of the six countries. Even though we had a military division within the GCC headquarters, and we collaborated with it with regards to telecommunication issues, especially signal interferences of military ships roaming the gulf waters, and other related issues; the subject of cyber threats never came up; and they were actually not aware of any potential threats by viruses and worms during those early years of the internet popularity. It is understandable, as the phenomena of cyber threats has evolved more in the past 5-10 years only.

During early years of the 1980s and 1990s, most if not all the IT and Telecommunications network infrastructures were located at major government entities and large private companies within the six nations. They were based on mainframes (large computers) provided by few computer companies such as IBM (International Business Machines). These computing environments were closed with no on-line access from the outside premises, and no social on-line media and applications were available at that time in posing any threats from cyber attacks.

The proliferation of Internet usage and the widespread use of on-line connectivity has become the norms of doing business, and each organization either government agency or private entity are told to adapt Internet and online accesses as a platform of operations otherwise they would be considered not technologically modern and trendy. The demand to carry out online access using PCs, and mobile tools such as ipads, digital phones, etc., has been accepted as the standard to communicate with different computing network infrastructures within an organization. In fact, all hardware and software manufacturers are promoting and advocating these mobile devices and access technologies, and market and sell them aggressively. This is the wave of the future. But then with every good part comes the bad part: cyber threats.

The GCC countries were very under developed when it came to information systems and telecommunication in the 1980s and 1990s. These countries were highly regulated by government agencies and purely manipulative when it came to these technologies. There was still the fear of foreign companies and other countries penetrating their IT and telecommunication infrastructures. Government authorities felt they had to have all access and ownership of any IT equipment and telecommunication systems sold within its border. Even satellite dishes were not permitted during these periods and were controlled in fearing the impact of foreign broadcasting on its population. Ownership on the issue of many of networking and telecommunication equipments, were so restricted that a purchase and installation of a private telecommunication box (PBX), or a wire loop telephone system for business and home, must come with a permit from telecommunication authorities which are owned in that region completely by governments. Hardware and software companies which are mainly foreign ones, were monitored in terms of their sales. Authorized dealers needed to report on a daily basis any sales and to whom the sell. Regulatory systems were strict and authorities had full power to utilize any legal means to enforce their manipulative practices. During the early years of the internet, owning a Skype account was considered illegal. Internet speed and penetration was so backward, that if you wanted an internet line you would get a small bandwidth with such controls and such high cost that it was prohibitive and not even worth it to have. However, businesses and particularly multi-national companies operating within GCC countries needed internet and communication technologies. They had to live and survive with whatever technologies were available at hand. When it came to telecommunications difficulties within GCC countries, it was also not an easy or smooth operation. Given different interests and illegal practices of trying to circumvent monopolistic authorities in having internet and wireless access, airways were jammed with so many frequencies that signals were always weak or not available. Causes of frequency crowding and causing different types of jamming from international frequencies emitted from warships roaming the Strait of Hormoze, in addition to existing foreign military bases with their own advanced and sophisticated telecommunications systems, where the six nations were not able to control their own airways. The multinational military forces that come and go out of the gulf region have their own full authority to control their own telecommunication and information systems.

The big change happened in the 20th century with the advancement of mobile technologies, all types of PCs, and mobile devices, in addition to free calls generated by all telecommunication mediums such as Skype, Vipers, and others that the gulf countries with their telecommunication and ICT authorities have stood defenseless, seeing their grip on their monopolies disappearing. They are still trying hard through the newly introduced laws with stiff regulations and penalties to exercise control, but this is becoming impossible in a free for all information exchanges as the world is becoming smaller and communications amongst people is becoming more accessible.

In the years to follow, many GCC countries signed military agreements with powerful western countries in setting up military bases within its' borders. These military bases have their own information systems and telecommunications capabilities. They are so technologically advanced and powerful, that they are independent in their working environment and accessibilities to their closed network and telecommunication systems, the GCC countries are not able to exercise any control, and I would guess it is part of the treaties signed or their lack of capabilities. Either way they are not considered a threat to the nations hosting them within their borders. The good part about having these IT and advanced communication military bases installations is to offer host countries a certain level of assistance in intelligence gathering and other types of military support to enhance national security. This was then and in the past, many GCC countries now have their own unique approach and capability in using the latest information gathering, intelligence activities, and spying techniques which are available for a price from other countries or the commercial market. These techniques and software systems are mostly sold by foreign western countries and licensed by their government to sell to other friendly countries. For example, many gulf countries employ FinSpy, a surveillance spyware developed by a German company called FinFisher. The software program when installed at the computer control centers of the country's National Security Agency, can monitor all types of media communications, including Skype conversations, cell phones and even pictures stored on different mobile phones. It also can record all kinds of Voice over the Internet Protocol (VoIP) and can extract files from hard disks. The software is so sophisticated, it can monitor mobile and cell calls within a few meters and follow up with the location and determination of its origin.

Many systems are connected to the internet such as teleconferencing and videoconferencing systems, security camera systems, phone management systems, servers and system administration tools. Hackers would look for these systems and similar ones, and try to find out operating systems they can control and take over such as Windows or Linux which are commonly used for internet activates and connections. These operating systems as discussed, have their own vulnerabilities, and hackers can exploit them and launch their own cyber attacks.

Cyber threat has become the main topic on the agenda of IT managers, presidents of companies, or top government officials. The transformation that took place with computer technologies and the internet just in the past 20 years within the six countries of the Gulf Cooperation Council is unprecedented. The latest and most updated technologies are used. They are being implemented in an open network environment, thereby prompting unwelcome vulnerabilities and security challenges of cyber attacks and espionage that are not typical for developing and smaller societies dependent on sales oil and gas in order to survive. It is for certain GCC main infrastructures including oil and gas, banking, transport, and many other vital industries and services, are not secure from cyber attacks. The current on-going implementations of the latest technologies either in computers or communications which are linked and interconnected to the internet, bring vulnerabilities to cyber attacks. There are so many examples of cyber penetrations and damage done to these sectors of the economy within each country. A number of cyber attacks were reported in the press but many that are not, are due to keeping people from panicking, and not exposing the public country's infrastructures weaknesses. The GCC societies are not used to having bad news coming from inside and outside attacks on its' infrastructures. The governments' policy, which is basically in control of media and press mandated to report generally good internal news, but bad news of interrupted services or cyber attacks or any other bad news that make government authorities look bad are massaged, and if reported it would be with a positive spin. Most of the news of cyber attacks on GCC countries are reported outside the area, in the international press. Information is collected from inside sources within countries, and reported to overseas media and printed out.

GCC countries are not considered technology manufacturing nations, but rather consumer oriented countries. They have to depend on foreign governments and foreign companies to supply, assist, and install different technologies and tools in order to provide minimum defensive mechanisms against cyber attacks. To have offensive cyber attack capabilities, nations must have technological advantages and skills that currently do not exist within these GCC countries. We know that Iran for example has started a few years back to build offensive cyber attack capabilities. The GCC countries' educational systems are outdated and built on memorization. Teachers hired either in public or private schools come from within the developing countries themselves. Not long ago, schools within GCC countries prohibited the use of basic teaching tools such as calculators. The use of laptops, or any computer devises brought into the classes were not heard of, and if a student would dare to bring them, he or she will be expelled as being a cheater. This policy has changed now and many colleges and even high schools offer laptop devices to their students as an aid to their work.

Although, there are a number of colleges especially Business, Engineering, and Computer colleges and universities that offer Computer and Communication courses and degrees, the countries face great shortage in manpower with right computing and programming technological skills. GCC countries do not import, use, and adapt the latest technologies. Even skilled manpower in such fields are recruited from foreign countries. The education system must change within. Dependence on foreign workers carrying out the basic jobs to most advanced administrative jobs within the IT infrastructures both in the government and private sectors responsible for country's infrastructures, posses the ultimate threat to national security of the country. Although many sensitive government entities do vet foreign workers with high access to the countries' computer networks. Background checks on them are not done adequately. It is therefore difficult to stop anyone from carrying out an in house cyber attack or assisting collaborators in working with an agenda from a base abroad. Background checks on people hired is a necessary step. However, this issue is overlooked out of necessity, but then the potential damage can be great, and when it happens is too late. The sooner these countries wake up to the fact that we need to start educating and training our local indigenous people and bring them up to international levels, the better will not be able to sustain certain levels of security and deterrence against outside and inside threats from cyber attacks. This will require huge capital expenditures of local manpower and not just on equipment, building, and software. The levels of coordination must be made stronger amongst educators and decision makers responsible for the country's national security. They must adapt a recruitment policy for the local indigenous people to run computing facilities responsible for the nations' infrastructures. It is understandable that this policy will not be an easy one to implement, given the current shortage of skilled local manpower. But, by having this policy in place, it will give decision makers greater motivation to start thinking of building the right local skills and developing the necessary long term plans to have local manpower running countries' computing facilities. This approach should be similar to building the Olympic team in which countries such as Qatar are spending millions if not billions in building the facilities and having long terms programs to develop the national local teams to compete in international events, and eventually the Olympics. Until we take such an approach and implement the right policies, GCC nations will face cyber threats and ultimately will have cyber attacks on its' infrastructures that might cripple its' economies and cause not only financial damages but also to its' reputation.

GCC countries & Qatar Cyber approach

In order to understand cyber security regulations and policies of each GCC member country, I decided to examine the Qatar cyber security strategy, knowing well that it can represent similar policies and strategies of sister GCC countries. As mentioned previously, Qatar is a member of the GCC organization which encompasses the other five countries, and shares similar policies, regulations, and strategies on all fronts including IT, telecommunications, and security.

Qatar's Cyber Security Strategy was launched in 2014. It included measures, initiatives, and awareness programs. The strategy called for protecting and safeguarding Qatar's networks and people from cyber threats and potential attacks, at the same time ensuring an open and secure internet and computing environment.

As we mentioned earlier, these countries look at cyber security as a side effect result of having an open internet society, and therefore all threats and attacks would come from the Internet. They do believe that due to Internet applications, threats of viruses and worms coming through telecommunication mediums can and will impact computers and networks. Due to this principle, they decided to assign the cyber security responsibility in the protection of the country's infrastructures to Information Systems and Telecommunication Authority (ICT). This authority has evolved to become a full blown ministry but with the same top management, personnel and agenda. Similarly, all sisters GCC countries now have similar ICT authorities and with similar regulations, policies, and agendas when it comes to Information Systems and Telecommunications.

These ICTs of the GCC countries do not have any executive enforcement powers in implementing and following up on various government and private sectors that compromise the foundation of the national security of a country. All they can be mandated to do is to set up regulations, standards, process, and training. Even with these limitations of executive powers of enforcement, these ICTs have done a good job so far in providing the awareness to the government and business community of the danger of cyber threats and attacks. They conducted various seminars and workshops, and even introduced internet security awareness in the schools knowing well that the majority of internet users are those young people who are considered half of the local populations.

The ICTs work with the telecom carriers in regulating telecommunications frequencies, licenses, and operational processes within the framework of the regulations and laws in place. The telecommunication carriers are independent legal companies and some of them within the GCC countries have government ownership majority, and therefore maintain a certain monopoly. There used to be in the past only one telecommunication carrier within each country exercising total monopoly over the country. It is now more than one and in some countries more than three telecommunication carriers thereby eliminating the monopolistic approach, and this is a credit to these ICTs to allow other private companies to operate with the country. The rates of phone and data over the net has been reduced considerably, and the competitiveness of service and technologies gave the citizens and business community the ability to utilize the latest technologies provided by the world market.

The local telecommunication carriers within each country controls the main Tier1 ISP and the network allocations of IP (Internet Protocol) addresses to all its customers. They provide either IPx4 and IPx6 address space. Many government and private local companies have multiple IP addresses. By having multiple IP addresses where only few are used for business and rest are just allocated but never used. The hackers can search IP addresses and find their exact locations and can be used in a cyber attack. Additionally, hackers can use the Domain Network System (DNS) which every company or a government entity must have, in order to be able to be connected to the worldwide web. These DNSs are provided by the telecom carrier along with the IP addresses. DNSs can provide host of technical and non-technical information to hackers attempting to attack. The telecom carriers also have a Border Gateway Protocol (BGP) which is basically a routing protocol ensuring all connection by users on the internet have a clear path to travel and reach destination, and if a failure will occur in one route an alternative path will be identified. I presume the local telecom carriers do provide such gateway protocols to its' customers, and the ICTs, and the local regulatory authorities) within the GCC countries thereby ensuring such alternative paths are provided in the case of connection failures or a cyber attack discovery. Many of the Middle Eastern countries, including the GCC countries belong to the APNIC (Asia-Pacific Network Information Center). This center maintains the registry of internet numbers, and provides its members the necessary assistance and means of having clear paths in keeping the country well connected at all time. Similar registry centers exist for many other regions in the world.

For the GCC countries and in particular Qatar, it is known that cyber attacks are coming through the Internet by using email addresses not only in the use of the classical desktop computers, but also on mobile devices such as iPads, laptops, and digital phones. This cyber attack is called spear phishing. The emails and SMS messages which are sent frequently to various types of companies and people located in these countries however innocent looking they are, can contain destructive attached files with viruses and worms and when opened they are immediately launched. These threats are still going on and are large in number, and as was stated and reported in the media, such as the IMF attack and many other attacks where the viruses are released through the email phishing. These techniques have exponentially exploded and took on different techniques and ingenious forms. Many people fall into the trap of opening their emails not noticing who the real senders are. They are used to open the file attached thinking it is either a letter or some document, or even a picture, not knowing of course, it is a virus or a worm. These worms and viruses will initially when launched infect operating systems such as Windows and Linux, as well as others depending on the computing environment of the organization. From there it infects the applications further where hackers well know the vulnerabilities and weaknesses of each application. and we will further explore this in this book. These viruses and worms carry out the functions their codes are intended for.

The ICTs of the six countries realized the danger of cyber threats as recently a few years back and started to develop plans and strategies as to how deter, defend and protect their infrastructures and vital services. However, if you look at each country's strategy, it is easy to realize how simplistic their approach is to cyber security. The focus is on regulatory focusing on government departments by setting up emergency response teams located within the government agency and with a number of people might not exceeding 50. The cyber response team will try to find out through their intrusion-detection and anti-viruses programs installed, any cyber attack and move as quickly as they can to inform and rectify the threat. In many cases, these emergency response teams remind me of hospital ambulances, as they go to the patient when they get a call, and by the time they get to the patient, he or she has passed away from a heart attack or major physical injury. If they have not passed away, there might be a permanent injury in place, thereby allowing hospital staff to take care and bring the patient into better health. Similar analogy to the impact of cyber attacks on any computing network facility. The cyber emergency response teams get the bad news of cyber attack in many cases from the IT managers responsible for a vital company or government agency. The reaction is to dispatch a number of their team members, to help the IT department, and find out what type of virus or worm attacked the computer and network system. Their work is similar to hospital ambulances in providing first aid facilities and in this case giving advice and the tool kits necessary to clear the virus or worm from the system thereby rectifying the problem and bringing the system back to normality. This is the deterrence and defense strategy that is in place.

Almost all of the cyber emergency response teams and the cyber command centers, located within each country must have installed the required firewalls or intrusion-detection systems typically provided by international security firms or major software houses, like the ones discussed in previous chapters. These cyber security deterrence systems are intended to monitor the main Tier1 ISP, which is owned and controlled by the government telecommunication company. The objective of this firewall is an extensive index to block all types emails and messages and other communications that comes across from the worldwide web. The intention is to block or move these suspicious files and messages to a site for further investigation and clearance from any viruses or worms. Typical blocking can include access or messages that come from pornographic sites, and filtering out fishing messages coming across. But then the majority of other attacks especially the ones that are sent through emails with attachments that contain the worms and viruses are very difficult to block, and therefore each country is bombarded with thousands of such emails each day without blocking. The fact is that if you ask what is the budget allocated for the emergency response teams in each of the GCC countries, amazingly, it is small, and the majority of the cost is for staff salary. Ninety percent of the total cost of a cyber team which are supposed to protect the country's infrastructure is made up of salaries, and the remaining 10 percent is for hardware and software systems such as personal computers and anti-virus programs, tool kits, and intrusion detection systems. Therefore, the total budget in many of these countries depending on the size and economic ability of the country, would not exceed a couple of millions of dollars. However, when a major attack takes place on a vital infrastructures, such as the cyber attack on the giant oil company in Saudi Arabia, Aramco, the company which is considered one of the richest and largest oil and gas companies in the world, pumping around 10 million barrels a day, and probably has one of the highest budgets for the computing and communication systems, that could not stop a cyber attack. The company ended up paying millions of dollars to foreign cyber expert companies, not including advisors and other expertise, to clean up the thousands of computers infected with the attacker's virus. These computers not only stopped functioning, the data on them were already downloaded and then stolen. Similar cases of cyber attacks happened with the gas company, Qatar Gas, in the neighboring country, Qatar. These two giant oil and gas companies would likely spent millions to fix their computer and network systems. Furthermore, they will definitely have learned from this and placed in-house a much more aggressive cyber defensive strategy. The current and future budget will now be different than before knowing how devastating a cyber attack can be in their infrastructure. In comparison, the advanced countries budget for cyber security is in the billions of dollars for each country such as the United States, China, and Russia, amongst others. Of course, one would say that these countries use such a large budget for their offensive plans to monitor, spy, and probably attack other countries, but the fact is that the majority of the budget goes to establish the necessary cyber center and command operations which require a large budget for the hardware, software and local personnel. All of this is for creating the deterrence and defense arrangements for protecting the vital sectors of the country.

They have already started to focus on them in having specialized teams and protection programs in place. But as stated they are under the authority of the regulatory agencies with their recommendation powers. These types of regulatory powers are generated from the old guards of the 80s and 90s where controls of all incoming, distribution, and dissemination electronic means generated over the phones, internet, satellites, and any other information systems and telecommunications mediums must be under the control of the ICTS within the border of the six countries. For the past 20 years, these countries were able to some extent control access to information through the use of extreme regulatory forces, and now all the GCC countries have cyber law punishing those who dare to commit a cyber crime, if they get caught. The government entities monopolized the use and access of information over the internet and airwaves, and generates such close and heavy control where citizens and in many ways even companies have to apply different means, though not necessarily illegal, to access information. With the advancement in information systems and telecommunication technologies in the 20th century, such controls by these authorities have to some level been reduced. I still believe the six countries have the fear of information access there but it is getting harder and harder with the latest advancements in different technologies.

The GCC countries have come up with cyber laws in the past year or so, and have stiff jail and financial penalties. To the point that if one publishes a blog or tweet that is determined by these authorities to be offensive to the culture, tradition, religion, or individuals, or other social issues, regardless if it is mentioned in the law or not, but can be interpreted to be against the norm, then the law will apply and the offender will be taken to court.

Cyber laws are full of clauses determining what is illegal especially in the access and dissemination of information. Even illegal use of networks, information, and telecommunication mediums, and other access, and in such a manner as described in the law to be damaging to national the interest or interests of others, then the law will be applicable to offenders. The Cyber laws amongst the six countries are similar. The western media criticized the GCC countries in having such strict cyber laws, and that restrict freedom of speech and information exchange.

We will examine one country, Qatar, and take it as an example for the rest of the five countries that belong to the GCC. We will elaborate on some programs or attempts by other countries in protecting the country's infrastructure if they offer a different approach.

National Cyber Security Strategy & Qatar

In May 2014 the country was able to come up with the National Cyber Security Strategy realizing the importance and potential threat of recent cyber attacks on the infrastructures. Prior to this and in 2013 the Prime Minister of the country established the National Cyber Security Committee. The objective is to study and to ensure not only at a local level of the government entities but also on a national level that certain coordination is carried out and that this committee will be responsible to undertake such responsibility. Consequently the country's cyber strategy was born in 2014.

The National Strategy of Qatar is similar to the other national cyber strategies for the remaining five countries. If there is a difference, it is because of the size of country and the involvement of the number of government entities in promoting and implementing Kingdom of Saudi Arabia, which is a large country in territorial size and in population, and the largest amongst the other five GCC countries, which is more complex and would involve different stakeholders.

Qatar and the other GCC countries' similar national cyber strategies would lay out objective in protecting the national infrastructures from cyber attacks. The pillars of these strategies are: bringing out a legal framework with enough regulations to deter any cyber attack; developing and enhancing cyber protection culture within private and public sectors; and finally whenever a cyber attack occurs, all parties involved in the infrastructure protection mechanism, working diligently to solve problems and mitigating risks. These policies and national strategies initiatives are basically similar and on a smaller scale compared to western cyber strategies. They are slightly similar to the National Cyber Initiatives of the United States. Many national Cyber Security initiatives within the GCC countries have been approved by government authorities. They provide guidelines and roadmaps for cyber attacks' deterrence, defense, and protection of vital sectors of countries' economies. However, the issue here is how effective are these National Cyber Strategies?

Having developed a national cyber strategy is a good initiative. The next step is the implementation of this strategy and carrying out the necessary actions per objectives stated in its' framework. A particular agency responsible for implementation and follow up of such objectives and initiatives will need an appropriate budget to succeed. This budget has to be large enough to cover costs of firewalls; intrusion-detection systems; and anti viruses software systems to be in place on the computer systems running key infrastructures; which are identified within strategy framework. The budget also must be enough to cover costs of latest hardware and physical security systems to complement software systems thereby enhancing the levels of cyber security.

The second biggest challenge to having a successful national cyber strategy is in recruiting local national staff running the computer systems in charge of the country's infrastructures. These local staff should be well trained to have them qualify to be able to operate the country's cyber Center. There are a number of challenges and major stumbling blocks facing the GCC countries when it comes to implementing a successful cyber security center.

One of the most important successful parts of the strategy is shared responsibilities of different stakeholders within government and private entities responsible for providing cyber security to country's infrastructures. According to the Minister of Information and Communication (ICT Ministry) of Qatar, these entities and in particular, financial, energy, health, transportation, and other vital infrastructures, will have to coordinate with the ministry through their IT departments, and report any cyber threats. The ministry according to the country's national cyber plan is a work in progress in providing the necessary tools, antivirus programs, and other kits, to manage cyber threats, thereby enabling stakeholders within each entity to analyze threats and undertake appropriate decisions in protecting each and every infrastructure unit under its responsibility. Additionally, the minister stated that ICT Qatar is working closely with SANS, a leader in cyber security training. It carried out a number of training programs for government entities. Additionally, the ministry is planning to create an advanced Digital Cluster whereby companies working within the cyber field would create a cyber community, and carry out the necessary research and development in cyber technology hoping to provide the necessary protection mechanisms against cyber attacks.

The minister although stated in a recent conference on Cyber Security held in Qatar, December 1, 2014; that the country will not tolerate any attack on its' financial, oil or gas infrastructures, such as attacks are still going on and it seems many GCC countries are defenseless against them. Many GCC's infrastructures entities especially the ones in oil & gas are considered very critical for each country's continuous wealth and sustainability. Qatar's ICT minister admitted that the country is one of the most attractive out of the Middle Eastern countries to be targeted by hackers. This is due to its' wealth, geo-political involvements, and its' hosting the biggest sport event in the world, the World Cup. Recent attacks on the country according to the minister were on oil and gas companies in GCC countries which led to communication and internet disruptions for the biggest companies only proves that government policies have a long way to go to top or reduce such hacking rates . Although, neither the minister or other GCC officials have come forward to explain the magnitude of such cyber attacks on oil & gas companies, and what actions have been taken to bring back these companies to a normal state of operational. Matters have been kept confidential. One financial statistic has been released by government authorities stating that global damage of financial losses due to cyber attacks exceeded 400 billion dollars. No one is sure of the real total number and all are subject to estimations and speculations. Within GCC countries, cyber attacks have been blamed on individuals and organized crime but never mentioned by nations' of cyber attacks. Cyber security is considered by all government ministers responsible for information and communications fields as being vital to national security and sustainability, and there is more emphasis on this subject given the severity and increasing recent cyber attacks on the countries' main infrastructures.

GCC governments have been given ICT's sole responsibility in providing national security from cyber attacks. However, this responsibility has been falling short given its' nature. For example, one aspect of its' responsibility is coordination amongst government entities in receiving reports from entities hit by cyber attacks. These reports are then sent or stream lined to an operating room of CERT (Computer Emergency Response Team) in order to resolve the matter. This CERT is like first responders to cyber attack. When a cyber attack takes place in one government or semi-government entity, they will start making the necessary calls and if needed, dispatch an individual or a team depending on level of threat, with tools such as anti-virus programs, and kits, that may help clean out viruses or worms within the attacked computer system, and to bring back normal operational status. This unit also wants to make sure existing viruses and worms have not spread to other computers in other entities. This set up it seems is more reactive to an event. It does not mean proactive measures are not taken on smaller threats coming across the net and using existing communication mediums. It is easy to monitor lines and block any means electronically through the country's firewall, intrusion-protection programs, and anti-viruses that are coming from countries or groups of individuals. The digital signatures of these worms and viruses can be filtered and blocked. The biggest problem facing this response team

(CERT) is cyber attack from within the organization which could be an inside job.

An inside security hacking and cyber threats are easy to find out as hackers will leave their digital traces behind. Recently, we witnessed major cyber attacks such as the case of Sony USA. It is not known if the investigation is over. We know there is no concrete evidence as to the source of attack except accusation towards North Korea. It is not farfetched that the Sony's cyber attack was an inside job. A number of media reports leaked out in order to point out that other nations have shown difficulties in identifying cyber hackers. For example, one report in the media indicated the hacking job was done from a remote overseas place accusing North Korean of it. In another media report, it said the job was done from a hotel lobby in Bangkok, and namely from the prestigious five star hotel, the St. Regis. They also illustrate the means of doing so through sending emails using phishing techniques. These types of attacks would have been impossible for any government ministry within the GCC countries to proactively stop and to undertake any measures in protecting the countries' main infrastructures given the current cyber security strategies in place, which are not going to be strong and effective enough.

Qatar for example, and as reported in a cyber strategy document published by ICT-Qatar indicated the country is amongst "most" affected of all Middle Eastern countries when it comes to cyber attacks, and took place in different forms and types during the year 2013. If this is an indication, then we know for sure that cyber attacks that took place during year 2014 have increased many fold and probably were more damaging to the country's institutions and infrastructures. We have given examples of cyber attacks such as the one which hit Ras Gas, the country's main gas company. It is the largest gas supplier in the world. Other examples of attacks were targeted financial and educational institutions within the country. The officials at ICT-Qatar admitted in their Cyber Strategy document that cyber attacks are on the rise in the country, however, they are determined to ensure the protection of information assets to government, private companies, and even individuals. These assurances are easily stated in a document but very hard to implement and enforce. The Cyber Strategy document explains in one page within its' many pages that there are current efforts to be proactive in preventing and detecting cyber threats before causing major harm or damage to national security and other interests. We notice major initiatives are centered around publishing for example Anti-Spam Guidelines to reduce unsolicited spam (electronic messages) on individuals and organizations. Although these guidelines are important to have, we are not sure these guidelines have any impact on what is happening in the country. ICT-Qatar admits that the country had the largest number of Spam, more than any other nation in the Middle East. How many of those could have been prevented or damages minimized, we will never know. Most of these spams are emails sent to many people within the country with an attachment to open. They can be so convincing and deceiving and many targeted people have fallen victims.

The document states that Qatar Central Bank (QCB) issued and published to all existing and operating banks within the country a Banking Supervisory Rules. Part of it relates to Cyber security controls and for banks to follow. Basically, Qatar Central Bank is asking local banks to report any cyber incident or attack on their computing network. I am not sure I understand purpose of these rules if they are only supervisory and just reporting to an IT department at the Central Bank, which itself has possibly been under cyber attack. Banking computing network systems within the country are being updated by international software houses. Two of the largest computing companies monopolizing the banking and computing environment are Oracle and SAP. As discussed previously Oracle is an American Company and SAP is a German company. They both sell similar software banking products and compete against each other. The banking industry is considered their main clients and source of income. If there is a cyber attack or infiltration into banking computer network systems, Qatar Central bank and all local banks would first call upon these two computer suppliers, and try to understand what happened to their computing environment with the hope that no major financial or customer information have been compromised. Oracle and SAP are considered two large software suppliers that dominated computing scenes within the GCC countries, and in fact they have a majority percent market share in the major companies and government agencies that are in control of the vital countries infrastructures. These two major software suppliers who also work with the hardware suppliers, try to use their call centers, and dispatch their teams to any bank attacked by hackers, and report anything out of the ordinary, and if it has been determined that there is an attack, then an official reports to central bank, and of course to ICT-Qatar CERT entity for further follow up, reference and book keeping. Damage to attacked bank is done. The attacked bank will try to recover and get back to normal operations as soon as possible. Software companies as discussed do have the necessary expensive tools to establish firewalls and anti viruses required for these banks, but at a high cost. Most banks in Qatar are not willing to invest hoping that a cyber attack damage can be offset by a fixed liability insurance account or certain amount as a provision to put aside in case a cyber attack or certain fraud happened. So far many of the cyber attacks reported involved access to individual accounts or siphoning amounts from ATM machines, or an inside job of transferring money from one account to another with someone have access to certain levels of security passwords and other types of access granted. The majority of banks cyber attacks have never been reported to any authority and have been kept within local bank, for fear of losing face. Most banks when asked about such cyber attacks, would state they are coming from organized gangs who were able to infiltrate and access financial data causing financial damage. The bottom line the Supervisory Rules published by Qatar Central Bank and similarly central banks of other GCC countries are considered insufficient.

The Cyber Strategy document states that Qatar established Information Risk Expert Committees (IREC) in finance, energy, and government sectors. The mission is that a group of government officials from these sectors would meet once every few months, for a few hours, to discuss amongst themselves the latest development of security breaches and cyber attacks, and issues regarding defensive methods and ways to move forward. Also to update existing strategy and to follow up on any important and urgent matters. Therefore, their mission basically is to exchange information and then report back to their respected stakeholders or bosses about the meeting. Not being cynical or critical about the objective of the IT managers getting together once every few months and exchanging information, which is a good thing to do, but the question is how will they be able to prevent a cyber attack on their respective entities responsible for protecting the valuable assets of the country (finance, oil & gas, and other government major sectors such as electricity, water, transport, etc.)? What if there is an attack on one of these sectors which is considered a vital national interest such as the one that happened recently with Ras Gas, which is a government entity which supplies the country's gas to many other countries in the world, and if it is shut down, not only does the country lose major revenue which depends on in its' daily life, it will have ramifications on gas prices around the world, and many customers throughout the world will be affected. I would be surprised if a Ras Gas official, who is responsible for an IT department, or a manager can be freely able to discuss with other cyber committee members details of such an attack. The fact that many IT managers in the country's computing industry working within government of Qatar did not even hear of such an attack would be surprising to many. But if they received any news it would have come from outside sources. IT mangers in GCC countries mainly receive news of what is going on within the computing environment of their respected country from software companies working on bringing the computing environment back to normality. The most likely news came from within a cyber attacked IT department where operational people there had to speak and explain the hacking problems to software and hardware companies which supplied different products and equipment. International newspapers reported to Qatar Ras Gas hacking incident, and people started to know more about the attack. I am one of those people, although, being in the computing industry for a long time, tried hard to understand locally what happened. Still, until now we do not know the extent of damage on this vital company which is so important to national security of the country.

Within the GCC countries there is Saudi Arabia's Aramco case. Aramco is one of largest if not the largest oil producing nation in the world. Saudi Arabia controls one quarter of oil supplies to the world. The Aramco computing environment was compromised by cyber attacks. As described in previous chapters the worm that shut down the thousands of computers did so much damage that it is still not clear the exact amount of damage levels, and if it is the same worm that attacked Qatar Ras Gas. The two cyber attacks targeting two of the largest oil & gas companies within GCC countries are considered alarming. They are not unique, and I am sure there are many similar attacks which are not reported and will not be made public.

The most interesting case which we still do not have enough details of to prove if it is a cyber attack or not, is the case reported recently on February of 2015 in Kuwait, one of the GCC countries. Kuwait publically reported to the world media that a sudden power blackout in Kuwait city put Kuwait in darkness and with no electric power available to over 60 percent of the nation's citizens. The government media of Kuwait blamed the blackout on a technical problems within the largest electric plant supplying Kuwait city, the capital. Electricity and power stations are considered vital infrastructures for any country, and Kuwait like other GCC countries cannot survive without electricity. We still do not know what happened, the official explanation of the cause was a technical fault in power transmission. "Technical Reasons", the very obvious explanation if you really do not want to inform the public as main reason. Therefore, the use of a term as "technical reasons", would be considered a more convenient phrase to keep the public satisfied. However, even if it turns out to be true that it was a technical issue related to switches, the possibility of sabotage and the likelihood of a cyber attack are all considered viable causes of this sudden blackout of a major city with millions of people dependent on electricity. Power station switches are similar to other industrial switches that are controlled by industrial software systems, and as we discussed this in previous chapters, they are easy to hack and cause damage to power stations. We mentioned how Stoxtnet played havoc to the center fusion of the Iranian nuclear plant. A cyber attack would be as devastating to any vital infrastructure especially the electricity and water, which the GCC countries are so much dependent on and would not survive without, for a long period of time.

In conclusion we can state that existing GCC national cyber security strategies, and by taking Qatar's National Security Strategy plan as an example, are not considered as effective in preventing or even minimizing on-going and future cyber attacks. Although, good work has been done but progress has not been good enough, therefore a new approach, strategy, and a new model for a national cyber center to be setup and in new format than what we presently have.

Chapter Ten
GCC Nations Protection against Cyber Threats

Apparently the emphasis by many developing nations including GCC countries is to come up with cyber regulatory guidelines, policies, procedures, and recommendations for agencies given the responsibility of providing cyber security protection.

Advanced nations with technical means, namely the United States is reluctant to discuss internet regulations with other similarly technologically advanced nations such as Russia and China. Concern by the USA with this type of cooperation with other nations on cyber threats is the fear of disclosure of technical details with regards to cyber technologies. Each of these advanced countries has been stockpiling cyber weapons in the case of war. Foreseeable agreement on cyber threats amongst these nations is not easily achievable in the near future.

Wisdom dictates that these countries should look into ways to achieve much better understanding and work towards a treaty with regards to Cyber ware. Cyber security threats should be treated like any war weaponries similar to nuclear treaties and others. Many super powerful countries' assets, including the lesser developed countries, exhibit most vulnerabilities even though they have the strongest cyber defense technologies. Without having a cyber treaty amongst abiding nations, given any preemptive attack by one nation to anther could lead to a cyber war. We witnessed a strong reaction from United States government when they indicated that a cyber attack on Sony America came from North Korea. The United States must have retaliated as North Korea was engulfed into darkness a few days after the US government stated publically the intention of retaliation. Cyber Wars amongst nations are coming sooner than expected. Then they happen, it would be difficult to control when different worms and viruses are laying stealth in each other's computing systems and can be activated by a push of a button.

The focus on nations building their cyber war technologies to be launched on other nations are not exclusive to more advanced and developed nations. There are now groups that claim to have similar capabilities. They come with political agendas and represent nations intent on launching cyber attacks on other nations' infrastructures. The fear that a group such as ISIS (Islamic States of Iraq and Syria) would recruit hackers and programmers who are able to launch viruses and worms that can impact against the vital infrastructure of any country they are at war with. Current reporting recently in the media referred to ISIS's intention of doing so, if they were not already involved in cyber wars.

We elaborated extensively on the most reported cases of hacking and cyber attacks. The Stuxnet virus attack claimed to be the joint work of the United States and Israel, on the Iranian Nuclear facility was one such example. The objective was to slow down the spinning speed of the center fusion reactors or manipulate speed without having the Iranians in the control center know that change had occurred. This was the first publically known and vastly written case of nations launching cyber wars on another nation to destroy the country's industrial infrastructure. The Iranians had pointed to the attackers being American and Israelis. To this date the two countries deny any wrong doing with regards to this matter, and of course claim national security with regards to any information release.

Other examples are also reported with regards to industrial espionage using Cyber attacks stealing data and personal information and inflicting financial and economic damage to corporations. The attacks are not limited between the most technologically advanced countries, but also towards less developed countries, such as Middle Eastern countries, and in particular the GCC countries.

Many countries have installed special agencies that are involved in the cyber security business such as the United States and many European countries. They all have either intelligence or military elements built in them given the increasing threats of cyber attacks that can and will cause so much damage to vital infrastructures of the country. They have built different cyber centers not only to exercise defense against cyber threats but they are also are designed to go on the offensive when it is needed. They have the technological might to create and launch various types of worms and viruses. While less developed countries have started to build similar capabilities but with less technological abilities and are mainly defensive style. They are for sure dependent on existing cyber security companies such as Symantec and McAfee to furnish them with all the necessary tools available to be sold commercially. These cyber security companies can provide security black boxes to look for any virus or a malware signatures and block it from entering the computing environment. Current centers handling cyber threats within GCC do not have independent legal and authoritative structures. They unfortunately started as civil administrative organizations under the umbrella of Information and Telecommunication ministries or agencies (ICTs). Therefore, the weaknesses of these civilian cyber centers is their ability to exercise appropriate and necessary defensive mechanisms against cyber attacks. It does not mean that they will not try their best to promote certain international standards, regulations, and processes and pass them to related agencies and private establishments within the country through their cyber security response Team. As we discussed the Qatar case with regards to having CERT which is a center for emergency and response. Similar setups also exists in other GCC countries with other terminologies but similar functionalities. This team is responsible in providing an alert mechanism to certain parts of potential cyber threat when it is reported, and provide the necessary advice and recommendations on the right tool kits and anti-virus removing programs in order to clean all existing viruses and worms within an infected establishment. However, these units' jobs in responding to cyber attacks' emergencies is dealt with like other civil service emergencies such as fires and health outbreak, which are considered mainly reactionary to an event. The approach is not as effective given the recent reported attacks that took place on main companies responsible for oil and gas production and exports in two main GCC countries Saudi Aramco & Qatar Rasgas). A worm by the name of Flame managed to bring down the computing network systems for the two companies for days and weeks. We will not know magnitude of the financial damages.

Many computing and commercial companies are joining hands with the GCC government organizations to implement for them latest and most advanced protection, detection, and anti-viruses programs. They are trying to catch up with hackers' technical skills. Hackers have become so advanced with the help of many nations and groups financing them and getting them the best technical assistance. They are able to develop the latest viruses and worms and send them out into countries' computer networks by taking advantage of weaknesses and vulnerabilities in the application, programs, and operating systems of many of the computer software and hardware manufacturers. Cyber attacks are normal occurrences in Qatar and GCC countries where they are hidden and stealth in their computing systems without knowing it. If they get discovered by any chance, it would be too late as the damage has already taken place.

Firewalls, intrusion-detection and intrusion-prevention systems are commonly available in the market. They are designed and written by sophisticated programmers either belonging to government agencies or commercial entities with a mission to protect the nation's assets. They can in many ways effectively detect worms and viruses. Although friendly western countries with political, military, and economic interests with GCC countries do share their cyber technology experiences, and certainly some of these detection and anti viruses. Some of their most advanced technologies such as decryption methods are not permitted to be exported or sold to GCC nations, let alone to those countries that are not friendly or are potentially considered hostile to them. Certain detection-intrusion and anti-virus programs that can detect viruses and worms known and written by security companies are allowed to be sold to foreign countries. They are already deployed in Qatar and other countries within the GCC and Middle East. As these anti viruses and intrusion programs are advanced in cyber protection, hacking programs are getting smarter and more advanced and therefore it is a catch 22.. Cyber security companies will include these new viruses and worms in their intrusion-detection and anti-virus programs after the discovery of the virus and worm, but new vulnerability can always be discovered and a new code to be written by hackers to bypass any protection in place. An excellent case example is the attack on Sony. As discussed previously, cyber experts are still working on finding out what type of worm hit the company affecting such a large number of computers. The worm not only cleaned up the disk drives of Sony systems, but also disabled machines from running again. This is following downloading of all types of files and data, in which many of them have been made public.

What Qatar and other GCC countries are lacking is local capabilities to develop their own traffic monitoring and intrusion programs to detect malware and viruses. This is done at the cyber command centers located in many advanced nations such as United States, Russia, and China including other smaller countries. The objective of having local development is to have confidentiality and security for programs developed in house and not by those security firms. These cyber security firms belong to advanced countries and of course they are obliged, regardless of their claim that they are neutral, to release information on clients if asked. The argument that these programs are either sold commercially and or advised and approved by certain intelligent agencies within a Western country that is friendly to other countries implementing them, is valid, but then we do not know all the facts of its' reliability and authenticity. We should not underestimate the fact that many of intrusion-detection, firewalls, and anti-viruses sold to developing countries have been compromised in terms of spying and hacking. The current firewall, intrusion-detection, and anti-viruses should be able to work in such a way as to alert or raise an alarm to any intruder and to be able to block it. The question then if they are as good as they can be and every entity in the GCC countries has purchased and installed these system, then our vital infrastructures should be secured, right? The answer to such a question is obvious. The GCC countries are not capable to stop new viruses and worms from attacking countries or their main companies' infrastructures. They could not stop cyber attacks on Aramco (the government only oil company in Saudi Arabia) and Ras Gas (the largest government gas exporter in Qatar), knowing that these two companies have the latest cyber protection systems in place. The cyber attack was in stealth mode, and the worm could not be noticed and blocked resulting when launched in an infection of thousands of computers. Until the writing of this book, no information has been made available on the magnitude of damage to the two companies' assets. There are such occurrences of cyber attacks on not only on less developed countries but also within advanced nations. Take for example the United States, where many companies not only in the private sector but also the military and academia have been hacked and many data especially intellectual property information has been stolen and downloaded by foreign countries. In the case of the USA the blame is always on China and Russia, but more and more in China on recent attacks. China is now the main culprit for such cyber attacks. These attacks are occurring with more frequency in recent months and will continue regardless of having the most advanced firewalls, intrusion-deduction programs and anti-viruses systems in place.

Defense Strategy

When one asks who is defending whom against cyber attacks? Is it a government agency with a team of people sitting in a room who call themselves the emergency response team and are capable of defending banking, transportation, oil and gas companies, amongst other vital companies that are considered the backbone of a country? Or is the job left to the IT manager of each company responsible for protecting a vital infrastructure to deal with cyber threats. Is the response emergency cyber team only providing guidelines and recommendations necessary to set up intrusion and detection systems required against cyber attackers? Is this enough?

In answering all above questions, we will need to understand that a civilian ministry given the responsibility of protecting vital infrastructures of a country in developing worlds is limited in many ways. Although, it is doing its' utmost to providing measures to government and private organizations, however this is not enough and as we can see in the following pages when we lay out an alternative path. Civilian organizations hosting a cyber response team have done a good job so far, but with continuous threats and potential future attacks, in addition to huge gaps in know-how and technological tools gained by hackers and especially advanced hackers including both government and private groups, has made the job of this cyber civilian entity and cyber response teams extremely difficult. They have become more and more reactionary in nature to withstand furious cyber attacks with devastating impacts on country's infrastructures.

Many nations around the world which numbered approximately 30 mostly in more advanced countries have established some types of military and intelligence styles of cyber command and are away from civilian control. The reason is obvious. If a nation wants to protect its vital infrastructure, you do not allow of a civilian IT manager. Most of IT managers employed in third world countries, in particular the GCC countries including Qatar hold foreign nationalities, and therefore their agenda might not be as clear to where their loyalties lie. Complicating matters further, they are hired without having the strong knowledge of cyber security and how to protect computing systems. They get to learn as they go along in their existing jobs. The solution we recommend in this book will take the cyber security matter more seriously and in having a completely different approach away from civilian controls and into the hands of military and intelligence agencies providing a maximum push of more secure cyber environments for GCC countries, and similar to a recent approach taken by many western countries. This way we can enforce proper firewalls, intrusion-protection systems, and anti-viruses into main computer operating systems, programs, and applications to be hosted and installed by companies or government entities responsible for operating vital sectors of GCC economies. In having a centralized military grade cyber command center, a different set in terms of hardware, software, and personnel are required. A simple example, is for sure there is a need for dedicated and encrypted fiber optic lines to be installed to connect every vital sector's computer system to this central cyber command.

This agency then, run a redundant intrusion and detection program on top of the other ones within each organization responsible, will ensure that all alarms and flags are raised and intruders and hackers are blocked if not at the source of the attack but before its' entered into the country and causes the damage.

The details and road map for setting up such military and intelligent grade Cyber Command Centers will be discussed in more details in the following pages.

Small Nation cyber defense: Qatar

Qatar can approach cyber threats similar to other countries with vast experience in cyber security. The United States of America and the European NATO members have been active in this field for a long time. As a small nation with vast wealth and close relationships with USA and European countries, we will expect Qatar to copy the same exact cyber defense approach as advanced nations in the United States and Europe. Technological gaps and other gaps are clear and will not be bridged no matter how financially wealthy a nation is. Technological and human technical resources are major hindrances for any level of equality in terms of cyber defenses between developing and developed nations. Therefore, for Qatar to be able to defend the country's infrastructures, it must create a cyber military style operation. The United States' Cyber Command, and NATO Cyber Command are a few examples to examine and study, but development of such a center must have its own character fitting the country's capabilities, weaknesses, and strengths. The same concept also should be considered for other GCC countries who share similar characteristics of Qatar as a small country's massive vision for the year 2030 and beyond. Qatar must entrust this mission of cyber threat deterrence to an agency that has both intelligence and military characteristics with authoritative capabilities to interfere and fully be in charge of any computing operation either civilian or government entity that are found to be infected by a malicious worm or a virus that can impact a vital infrastructure and thus national security.

Sooner or later, not only Qatar but many developing nations within the GCC region and other Middle Eastern countries will realize how serious hacking can be on their vital infrastructures. We will see these countries planning and if they have not already have done it in creating and setting up their National Cyber Centers under military and intelligence commands and commands.

The current set up with cyber policy in Qatar is that top decision-makers have entrusted a government civilian ministry called ICT (Information and Communications Technologies) to initiate and set up the Cyber Command Center within its' operation. ICT does not like the term cyber command center, so it is names CERT for Center for Emergency and Response Team. This entity does not have full authority to defend country infrastructures in the way the United States, NATO countries, Russia, China, and others have. It's basic function is to receive reports of cyber threats from various government agencies and semi-government companies who are responsible for the vital country's infrastructures. They are jointly working together with the IT department of an infected entity and using the necessary tools available at hand to clear up the infection, and put in place the necessary guideline, plans, training, and procedures to ensure this will not reoccur again. ICT Qatar only interfere in the entity's infected computing operations when it is given the authority to do so by the entity and with its' blessing. In many cases such approval is not forwarded or given. The entity entrusted with computing operations of a vital infrastructure already would have its IT team in place to tackle cyber attack and infection. ICT would only wait for results of an investigation and correction action taken by the company's IT department in cleaning up the computing network from any viruses. CERT team then carry further an investigation to understand if other computing systems in other governments and companies were infected, and issue a warning and further steps to be taken with collaboration to clean up infection and proceed accordingly.

Qatar has identified over 17 vital infrastructures covering government, oil & gas, and banking. This number will increase over time. It must have prioritized a list and ensures which ones on the list will be given the highest priority when it comes to protecting national security from potential cyber attacks. For example, typically the intelligence and military are first to have their computer network protected as they provide to its' population the country's necessary safety and protection. There are a number of control systems that are computer dependent such as radars, multiple data bases, large mainframe computer machines located at the central data center, and the backup systems for such data center. Furthermore, the list would also identify major infrastructure sectors, especially the airlines which has its control towers and many operations which are heavily automated, and interconnected via its own intranet systems. The airlines is highly dependent on the worldwide internet to provide online services from booking, payments, boarding, and other relevant services. The airlines has its' own firewall and also has setup a data center with a redundant backup center located physically apart. The airline uses the latest technologies, and is heavily Oracle based in terms of software applications, data base, and HP based when it comes to hardware. It uses Cisco routers and various other networking devices from other manufacturers. The list would also include other vital infrastructures such as power companies, Kahrama (the electrical and power generating company), which is a government entity that controls and operates power generators for the whole country. It is also Oracle based, and does not have the same computing sophistication as Qatar Airways. Its' automated control centers are run classically using SCADA systems where vulnerability are known. In addition, the company is heavy in using internet mobility and thereby making it more vulnerable to cyber attacks and other major infrastructures such as public transport, which is basically an old fashioned operation. It operates buses and taxis to transport people around cities. Its' computer system is SAP based, as a competitor to Oracle. There is no railroad or metro system, but they are under construction and should be ready to operate within the next 7-8 years. Other vital infrastructure sectors are the government agencies that operate some vital ministries of Finance, Health, and few others. These government ministries are typical users of computing and networking, and they are becoming more heavily dependent on online computing and in utilizing different mobile devices connected to their websites. The use of personal computers and mobility are common amongst companies and ministries operating vital infrastructures not only in Qatar but also across the GCC countries. They are open and vulnerable to cyber attacks. In fact, many of them have been hacked and much of their information and data have been downloaded and compromised. Given they are government agencies and have limited budgeting requirements make them unable to employ the necessary sophisticated tools as we discussed previously to defend themselves. They are dependent in the case of a cyber attack on Q-CERT (the cyber response team) to rescue them with the hope to bring their damaged and infected computers back to normal operation and hopefully recover as much lost data as possible. Major weak links into the cyber defense approach is the financial ability in budgeting for the appropriate security hardware and software systems. Many vital sector companies either are turned into private sector government companies, or publically traded companies. Having their own independently operated computing and networking operations, they feel they can have their own fully operated computing environment and thereby capabilities to tackle any cyber attack. They will rely on Q-CERT's guidelines and policies in having appropriate cyber security systems. Unfortunately, these companies and also by the same token the existing local banks will turn to but the classical computing environment with as little cyber security in place as possible. We all know how banks are heavily running on-line operations in providing their services. They are heavily dependent on the internet. The numbers of cyber attacks on these banks are increasing and although we do not have public reports on such attacks, as each bank wants to keep this news confidential. Creating panic with customers is not a good image and the loss of reputation, in a competitive banking environment is not warranted. Many banks do not utilize the right firewalls, but use intrusion-detection and anti-virus types of applications. Firewalls are considered expensive to detect malware and block them, and thereby given the limited budget each bank allocates to its' IT department, we should not be surprised to have such wide spread cyber attacks on these companies and banks.

Currently Qatar and other GCC countries apply decentralized cyber protection. Following the identification of vital infrastructures and in the case of Qatar, 17 entities have been identified. Higher authorities would instruct each entity to install the proper cyber protection systems, and to have Q-CERT from ICT-Qatar for example to assist each entity and to interconnect with them in order to provide the maximum protection, detection, and rectification of any infection from viruses or worms. Unfortunately, the drawback of this decentralized policy and having civilian supervision from the Ministry of Information & Communication Technology (ICT) to take responsibility, is the lack of executive power of authority over the more powerful ministries such as Ministry of Interior and Ministry of Defense. These ministries have their own cyber protection systems and do not report to ICT-Qatar. The policy of Q-CERT is to provide alarm when anyone of the vital entities is hit by a cyber attack, and by invitation from this entity to help to identify and fix the problem through forensic experiences that exist at Q-CERT. This decentralized approach is the one existing for a long time in USA. However, following recent increasing cyber attacks on American infrastructures, the approach has changed, as discussed in this book, to move into a more centralized cyber command & control system, in which has a military theme to accomplish it.

The alternative for Qatar and other GCC countries is to have for each country a centralized cyber command and control center of military grade and to have all the entities responsible for vital infrastructures linked to it. The center then would have full executive authority to interfere and protect the entity from any cyber attack given the impact of a cyber attack on national security. One of the major difficulties of a centralized military grade cyber center will face is to find the right qualified nationals to manage and operate it fully. One would argue that what Qatar is doing in its' decentralized policy in protecting its' vital infrastructures is enough for a small country with a population of 2.5 million and size similar to Kentucky in the United States. I would argue that not only for Qatar but for other countries who are members of the GCC Council to adapt military-grade cyber command and control centers. Qatar's importance surfaced internationally as a key country because it has become one of the largest producers of natural gas in the world, with approximately 77 million cubic tons per year. This makes the country extremely strategic to world's supply of national gas. Qatar supplies gas to so many countries in almost every content in the world. Therefore, the world community needs to maintain security for this small nation and ensure that vital supply of a key commodity, i.e., gas will not be interrupted. Furthermore, the country is going to be the host of the World Cup (Soccer) football in 2022, which is considered the biggest sporting event in the world with billions of people watching on Television, and millions visiting the country to watch the matches. There are many other factors that would make Qatar take the center stage not only in exporting gas or hosting major football and other sporting events, but it is also considered one of the wealthiest and richest countries in the region, making it a target especially in times where many countries in the middle east are engulfed with wars and regional disputes. Qatar has undertaken an aggressive stand to support conflict resolutions amongst nations in many regional countries, and this has also made it a target of attack. There are those who just want to cause damage either with an ideological or political agenda. Cyber attacks already are happening on regular basis in the country. We should not be surprised that many of Qatar's institutions have already been implanted by viruses and worms containing logic bombs waiting to be activated on certain instructions. Small and developing countries are as vulnerable as the bigger and more advanced countries, and it is for this reason that having a strong centralized and militarized grade cyber command center becomes urgent and timely. The recent power blackout that hit Kuwait, a GCC member country, is an example. We do not know all the details as to why this blackout occurred but the country was in total darkness. All we know is what was reported in the western media to be a technical problem and could have been caused by a cable failure, that knocked out 2000 MW of power from Al Sabbiya power plant which produces 5,700 MW of power. The technical fault disabled the plant. Damage was so wide spread and created fear amongst citizens of its' small nation knowing that a major terrorist act has taken place. A power blackout damage can be devastating to any country. What happened in Kuwait city can happen to other capitals within the GCC countries if a cyber attack takes place on a power station. We discussed how it is possible to do so with advanced hacking. The damage as we witnessed in Kuwait city due to this outage of power had a huge impact on the daily life of its' citizens. Traffic lights stopped working, so did hospitals running on generators, citizens did not have basic home electricity and had to depend on other means to survive in a country whose citizens cannot live without air-conditioning. Thankfully, the airport air traffic operations ran smoothly and I would guess had an alternative supply of electricity. The country managed to restore electricity after borrowing main supplies from neighboring countries' power grids. The investigation by lawmakers is in progress and we hope we can get some insight as to what exactly happened. The message is if this power outage was caused by a technical failure, it could have happened by a cyber hacker in shutting down the power switch lines as we discussed. Jokes started to spread across the social media, and one joke caught my eye, which said that "if our oil is gone? I am contemplating getting my very first camel now". The Minister of Electricity and Water apologized on behalf of the ministry to its' citizens and claimed that the sudden blackout was due to "circumstances beyond the control of the ministry". The minister and other officials have the answers and will have to state the reasoning of the blackout to parliamentary officials, however the real truth will never come out in the public. Similar recent incidents happened in Turkey. It had the biggest power outage in over 15 years. The country was without electricity and the causes are still not known. The power cut started in one power plant in the Aegean region and spread to other power plants across the country. The two largest cities in Turkey namely, Istanbul and Ankara, were without electricity which added to the misery and financial losses of the country. The authorities are investigating the problem, and the three possible scenarios are technical fault, human errors, or a cyber attack. We will not know all the similar facts of the case of the power cut in Kuwait. This power blackout no matter how it was caused, places the importance on its' happening by a cyber attack. With all the wealth and energy power these countries have, they will be susceptible to cyber attacks not only from unknown terrorists but also from other nations that are bent to carry out wars on other nations. Final thoughts regarding smaller countries' cyber issues would include the problem of budgeting for a centralized military grade cyber security center. I am sure it will be one of the major items on the agenda for decision-makers, and we will discuss how important this is for a successful center. It will be a different budgeting requirement than the one currently in placed under the civilian department. As the military-grade cyber center now will belong to an Intelligence and Military Command, budgeting will be much higher due to its' mandate to protect the country on a national scale. The GCC countries allocated massive budgets in the range of one fourth of the total budget of the country's defense. This massive budget is divided between military and intelligence establishments. Countries such as Saudi Arabia, ranks first in the import of military hardware, and this also goes for other GCC nations. These nations spend great amounts of money each year on military and intelligence hardware and software systems. In the case of cyber threat and protection from such devastating cyber attacks, these countries must take the initiative from the civilian domain and into a military/security one and considered the protection of vital infrastructures as a national security mission. Small countries of the GCC with defensive cyber technologies that are dependent on the Western world technologies cannot afford to be relaxed taking the cyber threat lightly. It must develop a strategy to build, operate, and maintain a central Cyber Command that is more aggressive and has a militaristic style. The cyber threats are coming into so many countries that there is no exception. Hacking has become the mainstream on the internet, where so many websites have been created by certain individuals for hackers to list their hacking methods, and also to request to hire any hacker that would do the job of hacking at a price. Most of these websites are based outside the United States, but in increasing numbers they are becoming popular, and for a price between 500 to 5000 US dollars, a hacker can be hired to obtain email accounts, steal passwords, download pictures or files, launch a worm or a virus into particular data base in a country. Depending on complexity of the hacking job, the price will of course go higher. Websites hackers' lists are sophisticated. This has not been an easy job for law enforcement agencies to track especially when they are based in China, Indonesia, or New Zealand. Cooperation amongst these federal agencies responsible for bringing down these hacking sites has become imminent and important. The developing countries, and especially the GCC countries (Qatar included) are more susceptible to the whim of people who have devious plans or ill will to cause damage, as they basically can hire a hacker from the website list, or advertise their intention and a hacker will post his price, and then a job is commissioned. It is easy to hire a hacker and those do not need a sophisticated spy agency or organized government agency to hack anymore into these smaller under developed nations that do not have the sophistication to prevent hacking against their computing and communication infrastructures. The main fear by the federal agencies responsible for tracking and cracking hacking operations, not only locally but also internationally, is that terrorists always will be looking into ways to launch a worm or a virus that might cripple or cause major damage to the vital infrastructure. Western nations are cooperating mainly the Unites States, with its' European allies who set up a joint task force and strong alliances between the intelligence and spy agencies, to counter terrorists cyber attacks. These attacks are happening and it will be the next war frontier for those terrorists. Most people do not realize how easy it is for cyber attacks occurring and system penetration into some complex computing environment. Actually, the skills required to hack into a computer system does not have to be highly sophisticated. With limited knowledge in computer code programming in Linux, Java, C and C++ language, a hacker can take down the computer network of any organization. Therefore, GCC countries and Qatar in particular should have such a centralized military-grade cyber center with executive powers to look into such hacking acts and potential terrorists cyber attacks, and mitigate immediate and future attacks, and to bring those people to justice. The approach sounds simple, but given the limitations of these countries technologically with limited human resources locally, the job would be harder to implement. Self-dependence by GCC nations on their own capabilities and national people would enable them to be less dependent on western countries' intelligence, and big software companies to assist them in operating and maintaining a Cyber Command and Control Center.

Chapter Eleven
The New Cyber Command Center:
Military approach

To build a central cyber command for Qatar (CCC) and other GCC countries, we looked at different country's models, and in particular the Unites States, European Nato members countries, and also China. There are similarities between the United States and European countries, but major differences with the Chinese model. Qatar and other GCC countries must look at what is the best model to implement and take best the features that suit its' size, and economical and political structures. Many would say it should be similar in structure to the Cyber Command Center at Homeland Security in the United States and in other European countries, but on a smaller scale given size and complexity of countries. To support this argument is the current close relationship GCC countries have with the United States and European countries. We all know that GCC countries maintain strong defensive, economical and political relationships with each of the GCC countries. We also know given such strong military relationships with the United States and European countries, GCC countries can solicit technical and even implementation assistance from the United States and Europe to build a cyber command center for the GCC countries. The plan to build a Military Cyber Command Center in each country given the presence of all the American and European software and hardware companies which will dominate the technological platform across the GCC's government and private entities is being formed. Although such arguments are valid and convincing, I would argue that there other models of cyber command centers around the world, and we should look at them and understand why they are more suitable to the GCC countries. I would encourage those to look at the Chinese model of having a cyber command center, which I find more interesting in providing maximum cyber security throughout the GCC countries. Existing cyber measures have not fulfilled their potential in reducing the number of cyber attacks, and in fact, this number keeps increasing, with potential major cyber attacks on main infrastructures which will be so devastating that recovery will take time and the toll of the damage will be high, which these small GCC nations cannot afford. We will discuss the Chinese model of cyber security in next section.

Qatar and other GCC nations should each have a cyber command center belonging to one entity that has military and intelligence capabilities, and with full authoritative powers. ICT-Qatar and in other GCC nations' civilian cyber centers should be transferred to this military cyber command center within each country. An executive order coming from this military command center with a clear mandate to interfere in any sector running a vital infrastructure if a cyber attack is known and discovered. Following the cyber audit plan discussed in previous chapters, this centralized cyber center must carry out, if it is found any weakness in defensive capability of any vital infrastructure, an immediate intervention in any entity either governmental or commercial company, in installing proper firewalls, intrusion-detection systems, and anti-viruses programs in order to maximize security and mitigate any potential cyber attack in future.

We do not have to copy exactly the central cyber Command of the United States or any European countries, as the objectives of offensive, defensive, and deterrence will be different given the size and complexity of the economy and utilization of automation systems across government and private sectors in these more advanced and developed countries. America is considered so large as a country economically and militarily and massive in its' nature, and therefore cannot be compared to any other country in the world. For example, Qatar's model of central cyber command will be much smaller and will require less of a budget not like the United States and other countries which have budgets in multi-billions of dollars.

Within the United States there were smaller cyber command centers operating within different military and government agencies, all of them have been augmented and centralized. Although, the private sectors which operate critical infrastructures across the United States' economy were not under pressure to implement their cyber security systems. The United States government stepped in to exercise its' authority through the regulatory process in forcing them to implement cyber security measures. It also supported these companies through a financial assistance to incentivize them and move along the process of implementation faster.

Meanwhile, as we demonstrate in following chapter with regards to the road map to follow in setting up a new cyber security command center, Qatar and other GCC countries, must approach the centralization of activities seriously and to have intelligence and military approaches in order for the objectives to be achieved, not necessarily in having offensive capabilities which require advanced technical networking, communication, and programming skills which are lacking across the GCC countries, but the defensive and deterrence cyber strategies. This can be achieved in a scale which is not necessarily as advanced as the western countries, but satisfactory enough to minimize danger and potential damage of cyber attacks on the countries' infrastructures.

The Chinese Model

Qatar is considered one of the highest wired countries given its' small population within the Middle East. Higher officials in Qatar and sister GCC countries pride themselves on having highly wired societies that are connected to the internet, and they have taken it as a national policy to promote e-government platforms across all government entities. They are even recommending private vital industries such as banks, transport, and Oil and Gas companies amongst others to join in this open internet environment and interconnect to the e-government platforms. This policy is taken as a way to promote a knowledge-based economy, which is one of the pillars of countries' visions. Therefore, support not only from decision makers but also coming from major IT companies who are happy to commercially sell many of their hardware and software systems in GCC market.

Qatar's vision 2022 for example is to be a major player not only in the export of petrochemicals and oil and gas products but also in sport and other humanitarian activities across the globe, in addition to be a knowledge-based economy. It has achieved remarkable results so far in its' vision and has become the biggest gas exporter in the world, and also a major sporting platform helping the country to win World Cup 2022, which by itself is major success for a small nation no one thought could win such a prestigious and biggest soccer sporting event in the world making so many other nations envious.

Here comes the big question, although it is nice to claim to have the highest penetration of internet and mobility in a small country like Qatar, and I am sure similar claims are drawn by other top officials within the ICT industries across GCC countries, then why are we not having the ability to safeguard and protect our vital sectors against cyber threats and cyber attacks. Apparently, these same officials do claim that they are doing their best to protect the country, but they also do raise flags of prospect and the fear of cyber threats that come along with high penetration of internet and mobility that are spreading across GCC region. They admit they will not be able to stop cyber attacks and hackers from causing damage, and claim this as a tradeoff between open internet society and cyber attacks which cannot be stopped.

So what to do? Well, let us introduce the Chinese model of cyber command center, which so far has been successfully applied in a nation of 1.5 billion. If it can be done for such a large country with the largest population in the world, then it can done for smaller countries with smaller populations like Qatar and throughout the GCC.

The Chinese model is based on a very single principle which is to stop any incoming intruder within the geographic a border of a big nation like China without compromising the potential benefit of the internet and thereby creating a knowledge-based economy for a country which has become second largest economy in the world after United States. China has to have main control in a military and centric style of management over three main sectors within the information and communication technologies. We will notice three characteristics that the Chinese model is built on, which comes from having a cyber command center.

First, it has to establish iron clad control over the internet and control what types of software will be used within the country. We all know that Facebook, twitter, and other western developed social media are not permitted to be operated in the country, they are blocked. Only you can use social media of the internet created by local Chinese companies and thereby control is fixed and government monitors all traffic generated in and out of these social media systems using the internet. Second, China has its' own telecommunication companies that are mainly under control of the Chinese government, although some of them are privatized and their shares are traded locally on the stock market. They are still maintained and controlled by the Chinese Communist government. Therefore, all ISPs Tier 1, and other traffic is carried out over fiber optics across, and in and out of the country, and linked with international fiber optic cables. They are all under the control of the military cyber command center. This cyber command and control center has all local intrusion and detection programs necessary to stop any intruders coming into the country. Third, and most importantly is that hardware and software systems that are used by vital industries and companies within China and for Chinese government agencies must abide by the security regulations of the country. What does this mean? All foreign hardware and software sold within China must be inspected and source codes must be handed over for certification and approval. This will allow the Chinese government to modify the source code of any software and have them approved for use within China. This action is taken for security reasons to accommodate the security requirements of the country. Therefore, if there are any weaknesses and gaps within any software systems such as the zero day weakness found in many operating systems and applications sold worldwide by major software and hardware companies, then China will discover it and eliminate it. They are familiar with the fact if a hacker would discover such weakness, he or she will take advantage and hack into any system. In fact, foreign technology companies' products must be certified by the Chinese government before they can operate and sell their products in China. The last example, was the delay in introducing new Apple iPhone into China. The phone has a security feature and thereby the Chinese government insisted that unless Apple released the source code of this feature to the Chinese government, Apple iPhone would not be sold in China, which is considered one of the largest single markets for Apple phones. After six months of negotiation, Apple agreed to the Chinese government's demand. A similar situation happened to Microsoft Windows many years back. China is a huge market for technology companies if they are not in China, their market share will not be as good. Apple's phone components are made in China, and considers China to be its biggest outsource market outside the United States.

China drafted government regulations forcing all hardware and software technology vendors to live up to very strict security guidelines before they enter the Chinese market and started selling either to government or private entities. The objective is twofold. One is to ensure security measures and the maintenance of national security, and potentially no cyber spying or cyber threats can be generated from having these foreign technologies on their soil. Therefore, with regards to software and applications, the Chinese government demanded foreign companies to reveal the source codes to them. Second, is to reduce reliance on foreign technologies, and to encourage and promote sales and innovation of locally manufactured Chinese technologies.

Initial reaction by many Western companies who have been operating and selling their products in China for a long period of time is unhappy one. Western technology companies operating in China complained to the Chinese authorities and urged Beijing to review an existing regulation plan without success. Following the Edward Snowden disclosure of USA spying using the western technologies which were embedded with either hardware or software backdoors with various viruses and worms, the Chinese government have become even more paranoid, and this is understandable, and many governments should also be aware about this matter. The Chinese position with regards to its' regulations and procedures with Western Countries were reinforced and strengthened, and Western companies have to live with the fact their know-how and intellectual properties must be handed over to Chinese regulators before any sale or operation can take place within the country.

The strictest regulation came out by the Chinese Banking Regulatory Commission. The guidelines consist of many pages stating security measures for technology companies selling to all banks in China local or foreign. The measures or guidelines covers many facets of different technological products such as PCs, servers, routers, wireless products, ATM machines, and many others. They also demand that source codes for all types of software including databases, operating systems, middleware, virtual private networks, and others to be registered with government and approved with regards to having security clearance and certification.

Companies such as IBM, EMC, Microsoft Corp, and Hewlett-Packard Co., have been operating in China for a long period of time, and they have large numbers of customers across business sectors especially financial sectors, and mainly banks. The release of source codes of different high technology products either hardware or software have made these American and some European companies nervous, and many of them are refusing to oblige given the release of source codes would mean the loss intellectual property these company spent so much money on research and development, on the fear of having the Chinese pass such source codes to their local manufacturers, and it is a matter of time before they are copied and sold thereby creating competition and threatening foreign companies' market share and dominance which they enjoyed for a long period of time. Many companies starting selling their business in China to Chinese companies in order not to live up to these strict security regulations. Recent intention by HP for example to sell its Chinese networking unit has attracted many potential bidders in China. It is expected that many will follow suit. However, given that China is the second largest consumer market after the United States, many American and European companies might have to live up Chinese regulation and compromise in submitting source codes in order to be able to operate in

China. The foreign companies who do not meet the government guidelines will be banned from selling in China especially government entities and government owned commercial companies, and an example is the Microsoft Windows 8.1 operating system.

Many foreign companies have caved in and cooperated with the Chinese government in revealing their source codes and other vital security measures within their products. This is good for China to protect its' vital infrastructures from potential cyber attacks. National security is more important to them than having foreign companies operating and selling within China. In fact, the Chinese government would use this tactic to promote local Chinese companies to have a better chance to sell to government entities, and increase their chances of having a better market share. Many Chinese companies involved in high technology products have become as good as their American and European counterparts, and are not only selling well within China but also operating and exporting internationally. Companies such Huawei, Inspur Group Ltd., and ZTE are amongst the biggest Chinese companies operating internationally and exporting computing and telecommunication products.

China created the Great Firewall to protect its' country. This is similar to the Great Wall of China which was created and became one of the great wonders of the world in order to protect Chinese main capital cities against invaders. China's firewall is to screen every outgoing and incoming electronic media transmission and to provide the necessary protection against potential cyber threats from malwares and viruses coming into the country.

One of the main difficulties in implementing this Chinese model for Qatar and the rest of the GCC countries, that these countries have an extreme reliance on automation and networking in connecting its' vital infrastructures to the internet therefore making them susceptible to cyber attacks. China uses less computerized automation within its' network environment, which makes them worry less about hacking. There are similar examples, when the car industry started to experiment with introducing various automation and computer technologies into the operation of the various units of the car. I remember that my first luxury car which was a Jaguar one purchased so many years ago, which was fashionably launched as the most advanced Jaguar XJ6 car introduced in the market. It was filled with gizmos and electronics and a computer system that would make the car run smoothly with less maintenance and headache to the customer. The fact was that my car ended up going to the garage every other month for simple repairs which turned out to be major ones generated from failures in electronics and computer functionalities. That is why Japanese manufacturers for a long time, and especially Toyota have been reluctant to introduce electronic into its' major models line up. Not until recently they started to equip new car models with electronic and computer control functionalities which resulted in quality issues and ultimately ended up in recalls. Toyota as the number one car manufacture in the world has become a model for other car manufacturers and its' car production methodology has been taught in schools. With Toyota venturing into electronic and other high end technologies within its' cars, it faced its first world wide public humiliation and ended up in US courts. It had to pay hefty fines due to the sudden acceleration of many of its' famous line up models. Of course, the monetary issue is not a big deal for a big company like Toyota but loss of reputation was at stake and must have impacted its' image and sales potential. There is a purpose of making this comparison between a nation or a company adapting high levels of automation and a car that is filled with electronics and switches that are controlled by a computer switch system installed within a car. Although advanced electronic and computing might help a product to produce excellent benefit to consumers, it is also brings side effects and issues of reliability and safety. The same scenario with the internet. With all the benefits it brings to users, it also brings danger of hackers and cyber attacks.

Cars have been so computerized, the plan by many manufacturers from the United States, Japan, Europe, and Korea which are considered the dominate car manufacturers in the world, to adapt more automation thereby making cars semi driven by computers, and with less and less human intervention. Examples of such technologies are park assistance, automatic reduction of speed in the case of a car coming or speeding into a car just to avoid a crash, with actually the computer system that can take over speed and control the accelerator, and in the future even divert the car controlling the steering wheel. These technologies have become standards in many cars especially the SUVs where with the push of a button the car can accelerate uphill claiming a hill or go down on steep hill without the intervention of the driver. The driver has just to put his foot on the brakes if he needs to let the car do the driving with hands off. The same goes for the Parking assistant where the car will be able to part itself with a push of a button. There are so many benefits and advantages of adapting this new automation and making driving easier and fun for the customer, but also there is also the ugly part of the technology that in case of malfunction where life can be lost and major accidents and injuries can occur. Similarly, the country adapting open internet and having such high penetration of internet and communications systems, is that the benefits of course are realized in having a knowledge based economy and citizens are enjoying other benefits of new technologies which the internet provides in terms of information exchange and access. But, there is a risk associated with it, that it is an open field for hackers and cyber technologists with ill intentions either individuals or nations to create havoc to the country or company; and to steel, download, and damage data and information stored in the network system thereby disabling vital services or operations. Similar to cars having one of its' automated components that is linked to the computer systems failure, and therefore accidents happened and lives were threatened.

China considers itself to be a developing country similar to Qatar and other GCC countries. This is not exactly true as China is not considered as advanced as other Western countries, Japan and Korea in the adaptation of the automation in the critical systems such as power grids, and other machines that are controlled by computers and control systems. Many of the country's major infrastructure industries still rely on manual controls and if the sector needed automation to compete internationally and reduce overall costs, then the application of closed internet which called intranet is utilized in order to have it linked to the country's internet. This means this company's private internet is not open to the worldwide internet but automation is provided through a closed circuit, however linkage is given with strict control to the country's internet. We know that the main country's internet is controlled and there is the great firewall that protects incoming hacking and various malwares and viruses.

China is heading towards becoming an international economic powerhouse around the globe especially now that China has overtaken the United States as being the biggest economy in the world having a higher GDP than the United States. The country is so reliant on exports of its' various products and technologies that automation is inevitable. But, its' greatest advantage as we stated that control the states maintenance over the internet and this cascades into various intranets with state owned enterprises and various other companies operating under the total control of the Communist party.

Therefore, an open internet society offers a tradeoff between the availability and wide access to information for the citizens of nations, and threats of cyber attacks that can endanger the economic interests of entities operating within the country's border. It is important to realize any defense against cyber attacks in such a highly automated society is going to be weak given the recent advances in hacking knowledge and use of existing technologies. The examples illustrated in this book show cyber attacks on many powerful Western nations including the United States, in addition to developing and emerging nations that adapted automation and those who became highly connected to the internet.

The belief that these highly automotive and wired nations have a strong cyber national policy and those measures to protect its' vital sectors of the economy from cyber attacks, is now not a true fact. There is no such preventive defense, nor deterrence against the hacking as long as the connection to internet exists. In fact, even if you can have the strongest firewalls, and many nations do have them, penetration into country's computing systems is a routine occurrence, and we read and hear about this frequently. In many cases, any report of cyber attack is not a clear source. We do not know if hacking is an inside job or over internet. We know for sure that many of these hackings are done over the internet especially using phishing techniques as we discussed in previous chapters. Many nations speak of having national firewalls and strong intrusion-detection, and powerful anti-virus programs, making it hard for a hacker to penetrate, but then there is always the inside job of hacking by individuals or groups of people intent on their hacking missions, and we have also addressed cases for such attacks.

Given the China policy as discussed with regards to the internet and strict regulations on the use of technologies both hardware and software; and total centralized cyber command and control over a vast sized country and biggest population on earth, this would not stop hacking from taking place. Of course, for any hacking to take place over the net in China, it has to be a highly skillful and advanced hacking, and only would be from advanced nations such as the United States for example. Therefore, the majority of hacking, which is never reported due to the information and press control, are considered to be inside jobs. When an inside hacking job happens and a virus or a worm is discovered, it will be immediately contained within the attacked entity as internetworking between entities within China is highly restricted and controlled. Virus mutation or infection to other entity's computing systems would be eliminated on spot.

The difficulty of hacking within China stems from the fact that existing hacking takes advantage of zero time or date types of applications and in an EXE files of the operations systems. All such applications and operating systems within China have already been cleansed and any weaknesses have been eliminated under existing regulations of having all western technology companies operating or selling in China to submit their source codes and operating programs. Government entities responsible for certifying these western companies' products is actually the cyber command and control center of China. It will ensure all security risk and hacking weaknesses in any operating system or application to be eliminated before permission to sell or operate within the country. Furthermore, China has encouraged many local companies to develop and write their own operating systems and applications that would have the same functionalities as western companies' products. Lack of trust of western companies' products especially those of computing and communications, is paramount in setting up the country's strict regulations and controls. Given the recent increase in hacking attacks on nations and companies, decision-makers in China, and the same to other countries, have realized the important of setting up tougher controls over internet access and the use of computing and communication technologies in order to protect vital interests.

Richard Clarke in his recent book the Cyber War, the Next Threat to National Security and What to do About it, illustrated in a simple table with a score giving the dependency ranking of a nation on automation and its' susceptibility to cyber attacks. A nation like China has the second highest defense ranking after North Korea. China ranks 6 and North Korea 7, while the United States ranked 1, followed by Iran and Russia. Why Iran, because Iran has been for a long time adapting those automation and internet capabilities similar to other nations throughout the Middle East. Mr. Clarke stated that China has the ability to disconnect itself from the rest of the world, and thereby totally isolate itself from cyber threats. North Korea is being ranked number one because of its' limited internet usage and limited or non existence of any automation in its' critical sectors of their economy, where manual operations are typically done rather than automation, thereby making the nation less susceptible to cyber threats coming from outside or even inside the country.

This concept of having major infrastructures in China and North Korea less and less dependent on automation, is not the main key issue, the main issue is when these companies operate their main and vital sectors of economy, they should have a closed intranet system within a highly secured environment. If there is a requirement or a need to be connected to each other or to the internet, such a connection will be controlled and overseen by the Cyber Command and Control Center in order to ensure and maintain cyber security. Therefore, what is the status of the six GCC countries including Qatar? If we apply the same methodology of Mr. Clarke's table of defense and dependency, then we can place the six GCC countries in the same class as Iran within the Middle Eastern countries if not even higher in terms of internet connection within the countries to the worldwide web. These six countries are so dependent on the internet that most of their citizens (over 85%) are connected, and even the same percentage and that higher of companies and government organizations who are wired and connected to worldwide web. Therefore, hacking and cyber attacks are daily occurrences within these countries.

In order for Qatar and other GCC countries to even think and adapt the Chinese model of cyber defense meanwhile maintaining internet availability would require a fundamental shift in thinking by decision-makers. I do not foresee Qatar and those GCC countries adapting the Chinese model. This is due to China's restricted and controlled environment. Also, China is so advanced in their computing and communication technologies, that they were able to substitute western technologies with their local ones giving them similar and in many cases better capabilities. With regards, to internet availability, it is very much available in China, but its' citizens and visitors use the Chinese internet portals and companies to connect to the outside world. However, there are few western technologies that are permitted to operate in the country as long as they are certified by Chinese government entities. The Chinese models can provide a platform where Qatar and GCC countries can learn from and adapt. The Chinese model of cyber security's command and control system can be a strong consideration by Qatar and the GCC countries. Although the model will have challenges to implement within the GCC countries given the dominance of western technologies on the GCC market and the strong presence in every organization and company. However, on a government scale and especially on a centralized military grade cyber command and control center for the country, the Chinese model can be looked at in a favorable manner due to its' strong benefits in maximizing cyber security. The reason I am recommending this model over other models within western world is that Qatar and the GCC countries are smaller nations with a smaller population but have one of the biggest national resources with their oil and gas. The GCC countries control over 30 percent of the world's oil and gas market. In fact, Qatar along is considered one of the largest gas suppliers in world, while Saudi Arabia is one of the largest oil producers in the world. Qatar is hosting the world Cup in 2022, and this will add more pressure on the government to ensure that national security is provided to its' citizens and visitors, and that they have a safe and successful tournament. The World Cup football matches will be held for the first time in Middle East, and in one of the smallest nations in terms of size and population.

Qatar has so much at stake, more than any other GCC country. Security and specifically computing and communication security are going to be as critical as any other type of security provided by the country. The magnitude of damage cyber hacking can inflict on the country's infrastructures is going to be so devastating to such a small nation, it will not be able to recover from it in a short time frame. Cyber attacks by advanced hackers have been powerful enough to infiltrate existing firewalls, intrusion-detection and anti-virus systems. A cyber command and control model similar in nature to the Chinese model, which has strong regulations, can be adapted by taking the best aspects of it and hopefully adjust it to fit existing realities and capabilities within Qatar and the GCC countries.

Chapter Twelve
Road Map: The New Cyber Command Center

This road map for the country's wide cyber security is based on other developed countries' experiences that faced many cyber attacks and threats. Although, these countries are considered advanced technologically as mentioned earlier, they realized that without having a centralized and strong cyber command center with the executive power to interfere whenever there are cyber threats, and to take control over targeted facilities, to be able to ensure that no other computing facilities are in danger of having worms and viruses spread across and impacting other vital industrial and service sectors' infrastructures.

For Qatar as a small country, a defensive approach against cyber attacks is the only way to go. However, given the increasing number of malwares developed by nations, groups, or individuals; many of them have become available on the black market and for a price. The number of malwares increased over the years and have exceeded 400 million. Qatar and other GCC countries can adapt an offensive cyber approach if they wish. Many countries have considered this option given the recent attacks on their vital infrastructures. Malwares are considered weapons similar to classical weapons. An offensive approach means to take cyber wars against other nations or groups sponsored by known nations. It is reasonably understood that each country must take every step necessary to ensure that their vital infrastructures are minimally secure. The steps presented in this road map are recommendations that can mitigate risk and hopefully reduced the levels of cyber attacks and ensure that vital sectors of GCC countries' economies are operational and continuous.

Intelligence/Military Cyber Security Command

The first step necessary for a developing country such as Qatar and potentially for other GCC countries is to create a Command and Control Center with regards to cyber security. This center should be located at an intelligence or military establishment, with full responsibility to manage cyber threats. Currently, such responsibility is left to the Ministry of Information, Communication and Telecommunications (ICT) where a cyber response team unit, but not a cyber command and control center, is created to tackle cyber threats. This team unit has totally different functionalities and responsibilities. The unit at ICT is called CERT (Center for Emergency Response and Threats). This task of managing cyber threats and attacks is left with a civilian organization located at the regulatory authority is not enough to handle the increasing threats of cyber attacks that are endangering many vital infrastructures of the country. This new militarized cyber center is the new approach to cyber security, and in which many countries around the world including many developed nations, have undertaken. It is very much required to enhance levels of Qatar and other GCC countries' cyber security.

ICT-Qatar or the Ministry of Information and Communications has so far is done good job in educating government officials of the danger of cyber hacking, and have conducted seminars and training sessions, and come out with a national cyber strategy and country's plan. It created Q-CERT (Qatar Cyber Emergency Response Team). It hired the necessary skills mostly from foreign countries to operate Q-CERT. Its' location is at the ICT's headquarters in downtown Doha, the capital of Qatar. What is lacking with this approach of a Q-CERT team carrying out the functionalities of Cyber Command and Control Center is to have the executive power and responsibilities that go with a cyber center's functionalities.

Currently, the Q-CERT job description is limited to getting reports of cyber attacks. When necessary an expert or a team will be dispatched to the infected site for investigation, to determine what type of virus and worm hit the organization. Immediately a set of recommendations of appropriate anti-virus programs and tool kits are provided, where targeted organizations are left to tackle the problem alone. If it is a government entity and does not within its' IT department designate tools to eradicate any virus or worm, then Q-CERT will be able to do this given part of its job description and responsibility. Although such an approach is commendable coming from a government entity with limited functionality, damage caused by the cyber attack has already taken place. We have seen this happen in two famous cases with Saudi Aramco and Qatar Rasgas. Both discussed in this book. The Q-CERT team would advise infected entity especially government entity to install a proper firewall, intrusion-detection, and anti-viruses. The responsibility to follow Q-CERT advice and their recommendation on proper solutions is left to the entity to follow and implement. This requires the entity having enough budget to do so which typically requires time, meanwhile weaknesses for further cyber attacks persist.

Many would ask if a small country and the same goes for any developing country within GCC region: Why do we need a militarized Cyber Command and Control Center when we have such units as Q-CERT in Qatar and similar establishments in other GCC countries? Many would say that why can't we stop cyber attacks, and why can we only can react and fix any problem?

In order to answer above questions from critics, we have to keep in mind that in any Cyber Control and Command Center one important goal is to be capable of providing defensive mechanism needed to protect the country's infrastructure against cyber attacks.

We also need to take a look at the structure of Q-CERT and its' executive power capabilities in order to provide a clearer picture. Due to its civilian organization structure belonging as a department within a ministry (ICT), where there is a limitation on levels of executive powers handed down to this unit. This limitation stems from the fact that there are certain ministries that are considered bigger and more important than ICT, and therefore do not accept another ministry with lower ranks to meddle in their business and especially to interfere with data and network operations. We can see this scenario in other GCC countries. This particular model of Q-CERT also exists in GCC countries.

ICT, not only in Qatar but across the GCC countries, is a ministry amongst many ministries. Dealing with the other ministries requires coordination and cooperation. No one ministry has executive power over another one. As they all repot to a higher authority and in this case to the Prime

Minister office (PMO), and any executive power on all ministries is generated through this PMO office. In the case of cyber attacks discovered at any government or semi-government entities, ICT-Qatar would act as the PMO for an executive power to investigate into the infected entities to access computing and communication centers. Part of the effort to reduce the lack of coordination and cooperation issues between ICT and other governmental ministries and companies, is to create a joint ministerial coordination committee on the cyber security, and to report directly to the Prime Minister's office (PMO). This ministerial committee will get regular reports on cyber threats and attacks, and discuss actions to be taken to counter them. This type of coordination and cooperation at the top level is half way to achieving success. Still Q-CERT, which is responsible for monitoring, reporting, and assisting in cleaning up cyber attacks, is within a ministry as a unit, and not at the levels of Cyber Command and Control Center as recommended. This particular model within Qatar is similar in many ways to other models within the GCC countries. Unfortunately, the current setup of Q-CERT has been recommended by consulting houses, as they have looked at the European models of cyber units, believing that such a limited model of cyber protection is much more suited to smaller and underdeveloped technological nations such as the GCC countries.

The recommended intelligent or Military Cyber Command and Control Center would have not only executive power but also can enforce cyber laws and regulations on each company or government entity's computer and information networks operating the country's infrastructure. This strong oversight and with the regular auditing of each computer and network site across country's infrastructure's platform, will force any entity to implement the strongest defensive firewall, intrusion-detection and anti viruses programs regardless of the cost. For any entity either government or semi-government, or a company in charge of operating the vital infrastructure not to follow certain executive orders and regulations with regards to having the appropriate cyber defensive programs, then this entity or company will be heavily penalized and the appropriate changes of leadership will be taken, in addition to strong intervention by the centralized Cyber Command and Control Center, to secure the computing site.

Military or intelligence style Cyber Command and Control enter is needed for GCC countries and especially Qatar. The United States has done so by combining all different cyber units located across different government including military units into one Cyber Command and Control Center reporting to Homeland Security, with executive powers to intervene if necessary when immanent cyber threat or in the case of an attack. The United States is considered the largest economy in the world with, many privately owned companies operating different vital infrastructures such as banks, airlines, utility power, and railroad companies. Homeland's Cyber Command and Control Center still has limited executive powers on those companies to carry out any direct intervention regarding cyber issues. Only through those federal laws and regulations passed down by Congress and followed up by Homeland Security, that closely monitor and follow-up with computing sites of these companies responsible for vital infrastructures in implementing proper cyber security systems can be exercised with the American. National Cyber Policy during president Bush's presidency and followed by Obama, there were more than a dozen vital infrastructures' privately operated companies to be included within the framework of a new cyber strategy in monitoring and following up with those federally issued cyber security regulations in having the right firewalls, intrusion-detection systems, and anti-viruses.

Qatar is so small as a nation, in which all vital infrastructures' operators either transport, power grid systems, oil and gas, and with the exception of the banks, are controlled by the governmental companies or ministries. Given, this fact where Qatar's government has total control over these vital infrastructures companies' decision-making, a centralized Cyber Command and Control Center makes sense. With regards to the banks being operating independently but supervised by a governmental central bank, cyber security regulations and guidelines already have been passed to these banks to implement and follow. A number of banks within each GCC country is not more than a dozen with different financial and investment houses. Therefore, control with strong supervisory and regulatory procedures can be one way to monitor and follow up on the potential cyber threats and possible attacks. The Cyber Command Center through the government's Central Bank can play an executive role in having a proper intervention whenever a cyber attack occurs. The Current situation with existing regulation by central bank is to have a bank with infected virus or a worm attack to report immediately to Q-CERT, and to have this unit at ICT-Qatar report the situation and what possible action should be taken to remedy the situation and to clear the infection, and to provide those details to the Central Bank.

Q-CERT's mandate is to provide advice and a set of cyber security recommendations to virus infected banks and for the banks to follow up on these recommendations. The centralized Cyber Command and Control Center recommendation is to have an on-line fiber link with a firewall security system within all operating banks. All cyber security systems must have compatibility in terms of their operating systems' of firewalls, intrusion-detection, and those anti-virus programs. When a potential cyber attack is on-going on any of operating bank, an alarm flag will be generated through the on-line network link, and a joint intervention between both the Central Command and Control Center and the bank. The process might not to be an easy one. Various banks in Qatar and across the GCC countries consider themselves private companies owned by few shareholders and those traded on stock exchange, require board approvals for any major investments and sharing of information. However, given national security reasoning and executive higher degree decision from the Central Cyber Command and Control Center, all banks must do what is in the best interest of securing the country's national infrastructures from hacking internally or internationally. Just imagine a scenario were major cyber attacks not only on one bank but multiple banks with potential fraud losses in millions of dollars, disabling banks from their operations, and disrupting services to clients, and creating unwelcome panic in small nations where news can spread so quickly given the existing strong social media.

a) Staffing Requirement

This unit should be manned with a local (national Qatari) team, and no foreigners allowed to join. They should have extensive training required locally and internationally, and should be in large numbers in order to compensate for any departures or a major turn over. I am not being prejudice here against other nationalities, but for small populations of nations across the GCC and in particular Qatar where only 10 percent of total population of 2.5 million is local, we can understand the current practice of hiring foreign nationalities with computing talents. This is common amongst the many GCC countries. Only Saudi Arabia has a higher local population and can represent over 20%, but is still considered minority. Always, there is this notion that because we will not have enough a well educated enough national team to run and operate the military or intelligent grade Cyber Command and Control Centers, we have no choice except to go to the international population and hire those talented people to be able to achieve any level of successful operations of such a center. It is understandable someone will make such an argument but from security concern, it is the best practice to have trusted staff with a loyal following of the country and without a hidden international agenda. Many Cyber and Command Centers around the world are so automated with tools and kits requiring less human intervention, and more of administrative actions. There is always a need for technical people to operate and carry out forensic work on viruses and worms when those attacks take place, however we always can provide extensive training for such staff, and within a short period of time such technical staffing can be mobilized. The current status for example at Q-CERT where the majority of staff operating and manning the center are those foreigners from different countries, local national staff is counted on fingers. According to ICT-Qatar, the ministry hosting Q-CERT, local population is so small, and therefore, there are not many local people around with computing or engineering experience to do the job.

Given the above reasoning by ICT Qatar of the limitations of hiring more of local Qatari talent and having a plan of training and education for them which could have been done many years back and we would by now have created a good cadre of locals fully taking responsibility in operating Qatar's center of emergency and response team Q-CERT. ICT-Qatar, the ministry, does not want to call this unit Q-CERT a cyber center, but merely a response team responding to any virus or worm attack and in an emergency situation. When it comes to hiring and training of local national at this unit which consists of a small team of approximately 30-40 staff and handful of local nationals not exceeding 5 percent, the responsibility of doing so will be on other ministries who are responsible for bringing up such local talents such as the Higher Education Ministry and the Administrative and Training ministry. Enhancing lack of having motivation of hiring and training locals to be at par with expatriate foreign nationals are the human resource departments (HR) job at government ministries. Unfortunately, in many ministries across Qatar and smaller nations within the GCC countries with smaller populations, we find HR managers are themselves of expatriate foreign nationalities. This would make it more problematic to hire local nationals as they would prefer other countries talents especially from their own countries. Decision makers on recruiting staff for IT and Q-CERT team, are themselves foreigners, especially their HR managers. Although, officially the mandate to prioritize the recruitment of Qatari nationals first, unfortunately this national policy is not followed especially when it comes to computers and information systems. There is always an excuse that even if you have a potential candidate for an IT job, the HR manager will always opt to hire foreign staff for the reason of having more experience, although there could be a local national with less experience but with proper training, he or she can match and perform better than a foreign national.

To carry out this major part of the strategy successfully, there are few steps that must be taken in concert in the process of establishing this New Cyber Command Center at the intelligence or military unit. We can consider the following as road map to successfully have local national talented staff in operating the New Cyber Center:

The New Cyber Center will require a minimum of 100 local staff in different specialties from hardware, networking, software and programming knowledge, system administration, amongst other specialists. Although this number of local talented nationals of Qataris might sounds big for a small nation with such limited numbers locals, it is much more realistic and achievable.

The main purpose of having such a number of local staff is to allocate staff over different specialties to oversee different vital infrastructures' automation centers. of the country's infrastructures. Additionally, we need this number to accommodate potential turnover which is considered high in the computing environment and can approximately be 20%. We can assume that the total number is not achievable in a short period of time, however, it might not require a long time to get to such a number when the environment of recruiting and training its' feasible. With the right incentive plan of salary and benefit packages to be offered, at much higher than market rates, we can recruit a local national with IT talent and experience that is already in the market. They can be tempted to join the Cyber Command and Control Center.

b) Motivational Issues

In order to get to the required number of good talented locals for the Cyber Center, we will need to offer different levels of motivation to work and to excel. There is the ultimate driver for achieving the required results. We will need to offer two things, a good education/training, and good financial incentives. This specialized new Cyber Center must have one of the highest budgets within intelligence and military establishments. The cyber center must have the ultimate importance not just in its' mission to protect national infrastructures from cyber attacks but also in terms of priority of having one of the highest budgets in consideration similar in budgeting to purchase new weapons to protect those nations from foreign attacks. Local staff to be hired at this Cyber Center must have a different a scale of salary and benefits than the rest of military and intelligence units or departments. This is not only to facilitate rapid recruitment in offering attractive salary and benefits, but also in ensuring that no turn over takes place as such experienced and talented local staff are always in demand and at market price, they will move to other jobs.

Salary and benefit scales have recently increased for local experienced IT staff. A package of 20,000 dollars per month is common in Qatar, while in other GCC countries, they might offer much less, as the demand for IT talents especially locals is high. The New Cyber Center needs to attract local computing talents of those nationals to join, then salary and benefit scales must exceed 30,000 dollars per month. Additionally, bonuses would be given to staff and the team managed to prevent cyber attack and enable the center to perform with excellence. With such high salaries and benefits packages we will see a wave of young Qatari nationals wanting to join the new Cyber Center. Currently, Qatari intelligence and military establishments enjoy one of the highest salary scales within government ministries following the Emir of Qatar's decision to increase all intelligence and military personal by 120 percent. Therefore, a total package of 25,000-30,000 US dollars per month is common amongst them. When such news of offering a higher salary package to local staff to join the new Cyber Center spread within all military and governmental entities, we would expect many talented people to join in. With the extensive screening, selection process, strong training, and financial incentives, this new cyber unit will be have an elite unit tasked with protecting the nations' infrastructures from cyber attacks.

c) Educational Matters

Qatar has many universities and colleges similar to other nations within the GCC. For example, there is the University of Qatar which is the main public university supported and financed by the government and where local nationals can get an education for free. You will see this model across many countries in the region. There are also private universities and colleges that offer different specialized education and are focused on certain degrees. However, the responsibility of graduating computer science degrees in a large number is with the University of Qatar. Unfortunately, the computer science program was not available at the university a few years back. Many of the current local nationals holding computer science college degrees are graduate of foreign universities located abroad. Due to the lack of such degrees at the local colleges in the past, government would send local nationals abroad to complete such education on the condition to be back serving countries with the same number of years they were abroad. Every year the number of local young nationals who are tend to become art majors are more than science. This is because it is easier to graduate, as the students' objective is to get any degree and get a government job. In order to have a higher percentage of computer science degree graduates, universities must offer those incentive enrolment programs. Currently, such an incentive is not provided to move students from one major to another. Budget allocated for education is considered second to military. Therefore to offer financial incentives to young college entering into engineering and computer department programs would require special funding. Community colleges offering two year educational programs must focus on the fields of computing and information systems. Unfortunately, many of local universities and colleges do not offer free training programs or night courses in computer science, which can create further limitations in the development of required extra skills. These training programs should be offered for free to young Qatari graduates and for one year or so, with even allowances offered and guarantees for jobs if potential talent is found and can be part of new Cyber Command Center. Unfortunately, there is only one major university in Qatar offering free education to local nationals, which is the Qatar University. Night training or specialized training programs in the computing and information systems are not provided. Private universities and colleges located in

Qatar Foundation and across the country do not even have such night or hours of training programs. Even if they can offer such educational or training programs, they will charge students high fees. This type of financial liability is not conducive to many young Qatari graduates who are starting their working career and looking forward to save spend money on getting either married or enjoying their salary by spending it all, as many of these young men probably end up doing, especially on consumption levels of luxury goods. One way to get out of this, is to sponsor setting up these night educational programs by the military or intelligence departments or by those existing military and intelligence colleges located in Qatar and other GCC countries. Financing educational programs which in my opinion would not require much budgeting and financial resources. But, there is the reward of having potential young graduates in those computing fields which I consider an important factor in being able to successfully operate the new Cyber Center.

Set up of The New Cyber Center

This military and intelligence grade Cyber Command and Control Center should be equipped with the latest hardware, networking, communications, software, and applications technologies to carry out the cyber defense and deterrence required. There are requirements to purchase and install deep-packet detection-inspection boxes to be placed on the internet's backbone, and on any automated control system on any of infrastructure sector or company's networking system, therefore enabling the blocking of any malwares coming into the computing network system via the internet. Encryption techniques, and software applications generating encryption codes are considered expensive and require countries to have licenses from other countries who produce and in turn allow their commercial companies to sell them abroad. I remember when I was doing part time consulting for the Qatari Foreign Ministry, that there was a requirement to have encryption on the communication and telecommunication network of ministry and its' worldwide telecommunication connections with embassies scattered internationally. The challenge was that all communication gears either telephones, faxes, or computers which are used to send and receive messages, letters, or having telecommunication abilities, were not secure and open to hackers and espionage. Most of those equipments with encryption systems are sold by western countries and were not allowed to be purchased by small nations although friendly to them. Therefore, the task was left to install secure equipment and encryption systems that I know for sure were hacked and spying on those could be done easily by nations who supplied them. For a small country one would think that maybe the issue of having a highly secured communication is not as relevant given not much classified information is there. But, as the country has taken prominence and importance locally and internationally given its' gas and oil wealth, the expansion of its' economy and political reach, it is apparent some type of secure communication is needed. So, we first asked suppliers of telecommunications and different hardware companies operating in countries such as Cisco and Motorola, if they could provide us with the required secure communications. The answer is yes they can and they would encrypt every communication coming and going out with their encryption techniques and the latest methodology. The only issue is that these are American companies and also the same goes with

European products. How can we trust them, and even if communications are encrypted they still can listen to the algorithms to decrypt those already well known to spy agencies within the United States and throughout Europe. So, my quest began to find out if these countries who have the authority to ask their commercial companies operating in Qatar and internationally can sell their products to government agencies, or if we could get the algorithm for encryption to be provided in a secure environment only for the country. Apparently, this was not possible, and potentially officials at the ministry were informed that nothing is secure with the current systems even with the encryption of communications between the ministry's headquarters and different embassies scattered around the globe due to the lack of owning encryption and decryption algorithms. The only secure method is to do it the old fashioned way. If an important message has to be delivered, it mostly carried out by hand to the intended receiver. Nothing is secure over the lines as explained to the top authorities at the ministry. Also, informed officials that the American National Security Agency (NSA) and other Spy agencies around the world have the ability to listen in to all types of communications. These spy agencies have sophisticated decryption technologies for any encrypted message and advanced translation tools utilizing powerful computers with artificial intelligence programs. Therefore, there is no message phone call, internet, faxes, or any medium of communication that is not listens to or analyzed, and stored away.

In order to get the best software and hardware technologies, and products for this new center, there should be ample budgeting capabilities. There must be an Independent budgeting that is out of control of bureaucracies from Ministry of Finance and other budgeting controlled agencies across the country. The intelligence or military establishment hosting the new Cyber Command and Control Center should be able to accommodate purchasing of all required products and technologies, and on top of it all, offer one of the highest salaries and incentives, therefore maintaining the latest technologies and best human resources. I would suggest that the salary scale be double any salary scale available around and if one government entity offers higher, this new cyber unit will double that amount. This is plus all other financial incentives such as yearly bonuses, and gratuities. All this would require a large yearly budget, and we can see how the United States and European countries, and other nations who created their Cyber Command Centers have such huge budgets in the billions of dollars realizing that with the abundant financial resources countries can provide the best mechanism of cyber protection. The GCC countries including Qatar spent billions of dollars on military hardware and training, and this spending is not under the control of any civilian bureaucracies of budget controls. Therefore, the logic goes that if military and intelligence authorities are in charge of protecting our country including our vital infrastructures, then why not treat cyber threat in same class as other threats harming the country's national security? This is why this new Cyber Command and Control Center has to be within a military establishment. Unfortunately, we have seen how civilian government entities have been budget controlled and in many ways refused certain allocations of funding and hiring of new personal, while military and intelligence entities enjoyed unlimited requested budget and human resources. This is not only for Qatar but across the GCC countries. I can sympathize with officials at Q-ICT who are in charge of budget negotiation every year for their Q-CERT unit. It must be totally frustrating to do so with the Ministry of Finance, who always in cut and the reduction mode when it comes funding new hardware and software systems, in addition to manpower. This is the current Q-CERT unit responsible for protecting the country's vital infrastructures of cyber attacks.

Having the right budget and getting all that is needed in terms of resources either technologies or human, is an ultimate source of success in creating the new Cyber Center. The importance of this budget allocation will be realized when there is a cyber attack that would disrupt and disable a vital infrastructure within the country. Only then decision-makers would realize this important issue and maybe they can pay attention to it. Unfortunately, the GCC countries and decision-makers have become more reactionary to the events and disasters, and we must move quickly into thinking and planning processes to be more proactive. The urgency of this matter lies within the highest authorities and decision makers of the country. Realization and awareness of those potential cyber threats that can devastate the country's vital sectors must be highly emphasized to such decision makers with examples and scenarios. Until such efforts take place, it is a common belief that any type of cyber attack and hacking is not really considered a threat to infrastructures of the country, and therefore we may not need to take this extreme case of a Militarized Cyber Command and Control Center and spend more money. Therefore, the current set up we have is enough. This logic is short sighted given all the reasons illustrated in this book.

I was impressed to see Qatar's highest officials in the intelligence and head of national intelligence agency, attending many computer and information systems seminars and conferences. In fact, I noticed he attended many of cyber security conferences held not only within the country but for sure internationally. This means attention is given to those cyber threats by top officials from military and intelligence in GCC countries. I am providing additional steps and a road map in this book to take such awareness and other steps taken by those intelligence and military entities to a much higher level in creating a new Cyber Command and Control Center, and giving it full executive power and the required financial resources to achieve the required goals in providing the country's defense and deterrence policy against cyber attacks.

One major hurdle

GCC countries are small in terms of having local nationals with qualified computing and information systems expertise. Qatar for example is small nation of 2.5 million with a small indigenous local population of nationals of approximately of 300,000. Only Saudi Arabia has one of the largest local populations which is able to produce through its' number of large universities, a higher number of computer and communication graduates. However, given Saudi Arabia's large economy and the size, the number of graduates in these fields still is failing short of plans and expectations. The shortage still exists across all the cities within Saudi Arabia, and therefore more and more dependency on foreign nationals to operate country data centers are inevitable. This is an even bigger problem for smaller GCC countries, especially when it comes to those IT and telecommunication technologies, let alone having a major cyber attack on the country's vital infrastructures. The new Cyber Command and Control Center will not be a silver bullet in having a defensive wall against cyber attacks but can minimize such attacks. We will need local nationals with cyber technologies knowledge at every computing and communication networking system responsible for operating the vital infrastructures of those countries. GCC countries lack the required programmers from its' national or local people. Unfortunately, the biggest university which is Qatar University with a student population not exceeding 15,000 students who are mainly majoring in art and other liberal subjects, with a few students in computer science and engineering degrees. The country does not have a choice except to depend on foreign expatriate programmers from different nationalities and countries, to run their IT and Telecommunication departments at the various government and private establishments.

We are not sure if the country does have a clear policy when it comes to graduating computer science students with an emphasis on programming and understanding cyber threats. The Higher Education Ministry is such a wide web organization that focuses on enrolling students in different grades and monitoring graduate numbers per the required market forces and the demand of the Labor Ministry. The two ministries work closely with each other in creating a plan of employment for the country's local nationals. The Labor Ministry would submit its' plan to the Higher Education Authority of what is required in terms of employment numbers within the country per expected growth of the population and those market job requirements. Higher Education which supervises all Universities and colleges within country coordinates amongst all universities per each specialization to plan accordingly with regards to students graduating each year. The universities and colleges then have their specific programs with their campuses to undertake the task. This planning approach misses a major task of where country requirements are. The job market data presented to the Labor ministry in such a way is not as accurate given the existing large foreign labor force, so the ministry is trying to understand which jobs that can be replaced by these young university graduates and those who would replace foreign workers. The majority of local university graduates are of art and liberal are majors, and they prefer to have administrative government jobs for reasons that are obvious such as Job security, the low number of working hours, and a less demanding work environment. There are a limited number of graduates that venture into private sectors such as banks, oil and gas, insurance companies, and tourisms, as the majority prefer government agencies. One out of 100 are in science majors and potentially less than 100 students per year are in majoring in computer science and they can hardly do any advanced programming. These few people would require extensive training that would take months to enable them to have levels of qualifications and advanced knowledge in those computing and communication networking fields. The same scenario we notice taking place in other GCC countries.

Therefore, amongst the proposed new Cyber Command and Control Center they need to recruit the brightest graduates either from local markets and universities, and actually scout for them early on, giving those incentives to join. This step has been taken by many nations not only the advanced ones but also those less developed ones. For example, the estimated number of people working with the Unites States' Cyber Command Center is approximately over 3000. In North Korea, the number of technical people involved in cyber defensive and offensive activities is over the 700. Even larger numbers of staff are employed at Cyber Command Centers in the highest populated countries such as India and China.

The new recruit must have extensive training either locally or internationally to be qualified programmers, and cyber technology specialists. Initially, we should have a minimum of 100 such students, as few might drop out and not less than 50 to be always available at the new Cyber Center. The second step is ensure that these new recruits have clearance and credentials with regards to national security. Third, there should not be and it is totally prohibited to hire any foreign national of any caliber, in any necessity regardless, including international consultants. Forth, the new Cyber Command Center should report to the highest authority in government military or intelligence echelon, so the quickest action can be taken and with that full authority.

Country-Wide Cyber Security Audit & Upgrade

One of the major recommendations in terms of having a good cyber security strategy is to know what you have now. Having a national strategy is good, but then we will need to audit what we have across government agencies and those semi government entities and companies operating our vital infrastructures. This is to understand how effective is our cyber security at this stage. This auditing process is considered a key element of any strategy, to be followed by an upgraded strategy to close the loopholes and gaps of those cyber security weaknesses thus mitigating risk and providing minimum protection against cyber attacks. The task of such auditing is typically given to Ministry of Information and Communications across GCC nations. However, we have such auditing processes fall short of its objectives. If an cyber audit is done then an updating of hardware and software technologies to bridge any gaps should be done in timely manners. If no auditing has taken place within the country, then one of the first tasks of this new Cyber Command and Control Center is to carry out such cyber auditing across all government and private companies operating the vital sectors, and to provide detailed reports to top officials, with budget requirements and human resources so a plan can be developed and followed up closely as part of an overall strategy for setting up this new Cyber Center.

It is my understanding that the majority of government entities and semi government companies operate one out of the four major software and hardware companies, including Oracle, IBM, Cisco, HP, SAP, and Microsoft. These companies are the main dominate players in hardware and software technologies across the GCC countries. They have and should be requested to furnish the new center with sold and supplied technologies to various government and private organizations operating those vital sectors. The audit program is by itself a lengthy process and should be managed by a team of audit experts, and in this case given the shortage of cyber and security audit professionals within Qatar and similarly in the other GCC countries, it is therefore recommended that a joint team to be established by selecting one of most well-known audit companies around the world, and embedded with local nationals who have experiences in the fields of computing and information systems and in particular cyber technologies, where many of them hold positions in the IT domain within the country and can be solicited to help in the auditing process.

It is necessary to bring government and semi government entities to set up and install the latest firewalls not only on their main computer systems but also to ensure proper anti-viruses and firewalls are on them if they are connected to internet. It is my understanding that an audit of existing software, hardware, and networking systems in terms of numbers and types have taken place many years back, but a comprehensive security audit program for computing environment for vital infrastructures of the country has not been done in Qatar.

In this cyber security auditing program the role of ICT Qatar as the regulatory authority of information and communication systems is vital, although we are not sure of how much executive powers they have in handling this matter given the sensitivities of the computing environment in certain critical infrastructures of the country. Therefore as indicated in the road map where if ICT Qatar is not given such executive power to carry out cyber security audit then the recommended Centralized Cyber Command at the military or intelligence agency should have such power, and I am sure that industries and service sectors running the vital sectors of economy would comply and enable those cyber security auditors and forensic experts to uncover any potential cyber threats and act accordingly. This is first an important step in addition to all other steps and recommendations illustrated in the road map.

Chapter Thirteen
GCC nations: Cyber Command Centers: Final thoughts

Not only does Qatar have a center hosting an emergency response team (Q-CERT) to tackle cyber attacks, other GCC countries have already established or in the process of doing so. As demonstrated in the previous chapters by having a cyber unit within the Ministry of Information and Communication in the GCC countries is not enough and will not be effective. Although, the GCC Council has not been at same level of achievement as the EU given the social, economical, and cultural differences, it has progressed on many fronts, and it is now time to move into achieving one more feet, which is to set up a military grade Cyber Command and Control Center, and to be linked with each GCC country's Cyber Command and Control Centers. GCC countries are capable in setting up this center and Qatar can lead such a process given how much is at stake in coming years and important of national security and operations of its vital infrastructures.

The European Union' Nato has an advanced Cyber Command and Control Center. The United States on other hand has similar advanced center. Both centers work closely with each other. The GCC Cyber Center should have certain abilities not only to provide cyber defensive but also offensive given the region sensitivities to conflicts and the continuous harassment by regional neighbors. The GCC Cyber Center must have such militaristic and intelligence characteristics as Nato. Each GCC country also would have similar characteristics but on a smaller scale. Having those cyber defensive capabilities in protecting the countries' vital infrastructures is a must. GCC countries are determined to link up electronically and on-line using the latest e-government technologies. They have become highly wired to the internet. Given they are now considered the richest countries due to oil and gas, they are continuously attacked by hackers as demonstrated in those previous chapters.

It takes only one virus or a malware to infect thousands of computers in one country and this can spread to other neighboring countries. A case in mind is when a worm was used by hackers who shut down computers at Saudi Aramco and Qatar Rasgas, two of the largest oil and gas companies in tow GCC countries. This is a clear example of how a malware can affect multiple neighboring countries. Any cyber attack by advanced hackers launching a number of viruses and worms can bring down power electric grids, banks, transportation, and other vital infrastructures not in one country but multiple countries. These cyber attacks might not be similar to the ones launched before, and they could be new ones that are not known to the current authorities. This time no emergency response team of one country will be able to restore the system operations in a short period of time. Imagine if one major infrastructure such as a power electric system of a country is down for days in the summer time when the temperature can reach 50 degrees, that GCC countries will cripple and stop operating. When Kuwait City's power electric went down for few hours for technical reasoning, it was practically felt by its' citizens that they were sent back to dark ages.

Hackers' launch of devastating viruses and worms would not come over the internet only as one would assume, but could be launched from within as an insider jobs, and we discussed how easy it is to do so in some of the examples that we illustrated. GCC countries have a large population of foreign international workers in residency and continuously arriving from all over the world. Their numbers are increasing and this has become a majority of the population in every GCC country. These smaller nations have to depend on foreign workers to manage the country's operations either current or future. The local population has become a minority. Half of each country's local population is not active in the labor force as represented by the elderly and children, Actual local population actively working in local market represent less than 10% of the total population. This means we have huge security gaps by having foreign workers from countries and with grudges and a political agenda against GCC countries. Inside hacking job represents the easiest of any cyber attack and we demonstrated how easily this can done. We know for sure that inside attacks are happening every day and in a continuous manners. Unfortunately, the GCC media do not report on cyber attacks given the political sensitivities and public determination not to alert those citizens. When an infrastructure is down, we notice that the government claims it on technical issues, and fixes are on the way. Unfortunately, not knowing the causes of technical problems exacerbate the problem and open the doors of all types of rumors and speculation given the wide spread of social media use, thanks to the internet.

Big government such as those of the United States, the Europeans, China and Russia, can allocate a large sized budget for military and intelligence agencies in order to protect their infrastructures from cyber attacks. One difference between the United States and other countries as we discussed is the lack of offering by governments the protection computer centers of private companies as federal laws and regulations which do not permit this. The case in point is the Sony cyber attack. While China and Russia can do this government offering, western countries' governments cannot legally. GCC nations given their size of each country and population, cannot afford to have its' private sectors mainly those that control vital sectors of economy such as banks and transport, and others, in private hands to manage their cyber threats and attacks. They will have to be included with the military and intelligence Central Cyber Command.

In having a powerful Cyber Command Center in Qatar and each GCC country that would be more militaristic and intelligence, with executive powers in protecting those vital infrastructures of the country, we also recommend that a similar military-grade Cyber Central Command and Control Center to be established for the GCC's Council and to be linked through secure fiber optic links with each member country's center. The Ministries of defense and interiors would take the lead and responsibility to proceed with a plan in setting up a centralized center and each country's center. As these six countries are neighbors and share many resources, and have the same background, it is therefore highly recommended that a similar Nato Cyber Command and Control Center approach be considered.

The GCC have been successful in setting up many cooperative centers and organizations. They regularly meet with various groups and committees to coordinate activities and share vital information. Having worked at the GCC headquarters for 8 years in capacity of Director of Computers and Telecommunications departments, and being responsible for coordinating and cooperating activities of computing and telecommunication activities of the six countries, it has become clear to me given recent cyber attacks on GCC countries and potential future attacks that would have major threats to national security that a military and intelligence grade Cyber Center is perhaps necessary and urgent. It is my hope this book will help in spearheading discussions and moving ahead the concept of creating such cyber centers in upcoming meetings of the GCC's military and intelligence top officials.

The GCC as a union has certain working structure full of bureaucracy, which means it will take a long time for a plan such as the one we speak of to get off ground. in Therefore, Military and Intelligence ministries and units must take the lead in promoting and adapting such a plan in a faster manner outside the spectrum of bureaucracy, given the seriousness of cyber threats on the national security of member countries. GCC countries are known to be reactionary rather than proactive when the crises occurs. The European Union' Nato in the past was reactionary in its' nature and for years realized danger of cyber hacking. Not until recent years when such cyber attacks starting to devastate the country's infrastructures did they realize protection against cyber attacks is considered protection for national security, and therefore they built the Nato Cyber Command and Control Center.

Therefore, it is prudent for the six GCC countries to be proactive in nature in dealing with those cyber threats, and to consider it a defense similar to military defenses against any attack on national interests. Not only to have cyber threats and cyber attacks the priority number one, and not to be left to departments or officials within civil and service sectors, but to hand over to military and intelligence thereby giving it the highest priority. When a GCC military-grade Cyber Command and Control Center is set up having all military and intelligent of six countries under one roof, ensuring proper strategic policies, guidelines, and measures to be in place, and for each country to share and to contribute with its' own cyber center, this would be an achievement for national security which is the main objective of this book. Meanwhile, if such a centralized GCC cyber center will take longer than usual, then each country should proceed with its' own plan, and Qatar is set up to be the first and others to copy and follow suit.

When we learn from others and if we consider how European Nato Cyber Command Centers build up strategy progressing towards creating the right structure in terms dedication to cyber technology, and with the extensive staff training to be able to have certain ability to counter any cyber attack. Nato managed to develop high level strategies by top governments' officials from presidents and top officials' levels in handing over cyber responsibilities to military and intelligence. Military and intelligence authorities are mandated to directly get involved in the protection of a long list of main infrastructures sectors. Nato's main cyber defense for example starts from the backbone Tier 1 type of internet traffic that is handled by the main telecommunication carriers within each member country, and abroad across continents connected via submarine fiber optics pipelines running under oceans, GCC countries are also in position to proceed with similar approach but this will require powerful forces and parties to be able to organize such a major cyber defense at the backbone, and only through a militarized Cyber Command Center and Control, we can see progress on this important front.

GCC countries have installed firewalls and detection-intrusion measures that would flag many known worms and viruses, but the majority have different signatures and can be penetrated through. Advanced hackers are able to change the source codes of many worms and viruses that are not available now in installed intrusion-detection systems. These mutated viruses and worms are capable of achieving their goals with ease. GCC military grade cyber centers have to have the capabilities to address such mutation of worms' source codes and are able to stop any penetration of viruses and worms. We know for sure that technology is not capable to keep up with advanced hacking, but only with strong efforts by GCC governments in knowing the dangers of cyber attacks that the goal of establishing such cyber centers can be achieved.

The work ahead of the GCC countries is not going to be easy given the nature of cyber technology and its' threats. European countries have given Nato the responsibility for cyber threats knowing the danger, and to be treated similar to classical war threats and therefore it must be dealt with in a military and intelligence style. GCC countries who have given responsibilities of cyber protection to civilian institutions must change its policies and move similarly towards a Nato style of considering cyber threats. GCC countries are basically technology consumer countries. They have to realize that their vital infrastructures are in danger if not already with the advancement of cyber threats and continuous cyber attacks in these recent months and years to come. GCC countries must act and act now as these cyber threats with the most advanced worms and viruses written not only by disgruntled individuals or groups, but by nations of sophisticated technological abilities that will cause extreme damage and harm to the vital national interests of GCC member countries. Therefore, national priority has to be given to setting up a GCC cyber center and for each member country to set up its' own center. This is for national interest sake and the protection of the countries' vital infrastructures.

The seriousness of the cyber attacks ultimately will force many of the GCC countries to consider the suggestions presented in this book, and in particular the aspect of having cyber security in protecting the national interests and infrastructures. Qatar given its' importance to the world, and taking center stage amongst the GCC countries would be a good example in setting up its' own Cyber Command and Control Center. I hope this military-grade cyber center will be established in near future and in a short period of time given the threat seriousness of cyber attacks.

Glossary

Viruses and Worms

They are codes written by programmers either as solo programs or a document attached to an email, that infects computers and other networked devices depending on the intention they are written for.

Spearhead Phishing

It is a type of email send to a target with a link or a file attached and the request to open it, and when it is opened the worm and virus is launched and activated.

Trojan Horses

They are viruses and worms contained in a file and typically look innocent but when opened it will launch a virus or a worm with backdoor access to the computer system.

Zero-Day Vulnerability & Exploits

Hackers discover certain vulnerability called Zero-Day, and these vulnerabilities exist with many operating systems, and software applications. Hackers will exploit this vulnerability and try to write the codes to have an access to the system. When such vulnerability is discovered, the vendor comes out with a patch fixing this vulnerability.

Stack & Heap Overflow Batches

Many vulnerabilities exist with software applications given there are hundreds of lines of codes, and when these vulnerabilities are discovered, patches are developed by the vendor, and the fixe will be in place. Also, if these are major vulnerabilities, then many vendors will update the software system with new releases.

Social Engineering

It is the use of the common knowledge and available public information either on the internet or through other public sources whereby hackers can use such information for reconnaissance purposes preparing for the actual hacking.

Botnets

Is a warm which infects computers to make them act like zombies and in the control of the hackers without owner knowledge. As the infection spreads to other linked computers, they are called botnets.

Firewall

A software program that can monitor traffic and keep out any suspicious viruses or worms seeking to infiltrate through the traffic coming into the computing environment. Many organizations implement them to ensure providing minimum security against cyber attacks.

Anti-viruses

Software programs developed by the security vendor for the protection of the computer system from any potential virus infection or hacking. When installed they can scan and clean any viruses or worms that are in their digital signature repository or data base. It can also filter anything incoming These programs are considered the first step for any minimum protection from any hacking.

Intrusion-Detection programs

These programs are developed by security and software vendors providing additional detection ability for any potential infection via any known viruses or worms. With the firewall programs, they become an effective mechanism in providing the minimum protection system for the computing facility.

Authentication

The process of confirming the authenticity of the individuals accessing the computing system by presenting certain credentials such as user identification, passwords, smart cards. fingerprints, and other means of authentication processes.

Tier 1

This is the main and big pipeline that is used by telecommunication carriers to carry the telephony and other digital media along with all internet traffic from one destination to another. These main lines are made of fiber optics or major submarine cables crossing many countries. They are the backbone of the telecommunication and network traffic for a country.

Border Gateway Protocol (BGP)

ISP (Internet Service Providers) use this internet protocol to communicate with each other. ISPs are the main telecommunication internet traffic carriers. The BGP protocol organizes the routing mechanisms between the different ISPs around the world, and ensure that all traffic generated by internet clients reach the right destination.

Distributed Denial of Service (DDoS)

This is one of the most popular of cyber attacks where a server or internet site is flooded with requests that would cause the site to overload and thereby stop functioning. These DDoS are automatically generated by robot computers. If any user would access the internet site a denial request will show saying unable to access.

Token Key

It is both physical unit as a device that generate random six digit number. This device belongs to the user and only he has the pin number to enter into the device, and when the six digits are presented every 60 seconds, the user then uses this to access his account after entering the user identification and password. Tokens can provide a higher level of security to users access company sites and popularity of RSA token is spreading in the computing world.

Backdoors

Backdoors are viruses and worms embedded in a file and launched when opened. The backdoor is a stealth program that would stay for a long time without the knowledge of the target. Its' mission per coded instruction could be from obtaining data to any other spying or hacking activities. The vast majority of backdoors are based on auto start and targeted Windows operating systems. These autostarts are located in the registry of the operating systems, and mainly in the schedule tasks, autostart folders, and register locations such as Run, RunOnce, and RunServices.

Logic bomb

are worms that are activated based on its' written code instructions. Logic bomb can cause damage to either the computer data by wiping it out, or to vital infrastructures such as power grids, and others.

Reconnaissance

A practice use by advance hackers to understand and have full knowledge of the target to be attacked. This can involve non technical and technical information. Social engineering and other vital surveillances are used to acquire as much information as possible about the target thereby making the hacking job easier.

Oracle & SAP

The two giant software companies who started their initial business selling business application and data base software systems to all size of companies, now dominate the software landscape of many companies around the world, and they depend very much on these software companies for daily operational survival. Oracle is an American based company founded by Larry Ellison, while SAP is a German based company, and co-founded by x-employees of IBM. Between them they have control over the 50-60% of the market share of the business software systems.

Encryption & Decryption Techniques

These techniques are used by security houses and other major software vendors to protect the data traveling over telecommunication and other media. The algorithms used for encryption depend on the length of the key used to encrypt and the complexity of the algorithm. To decrypt on the other end of the transmission a decryption key is needed which is only known to the user. The use of public and private keys are particularly important in the process. Encryption and decryption of text messages, files, and other documents are common and the user can commercially obtain them.

Domain Network Systems (DNS)

The DNS is provided by the internet carrier to its' client where they can have multiple IP (Internet Protocol) addresses. Therefore, within the DNS provided to a company, many IP addresses can be reserved and used by the client to rout the company internet traffic.

Stealth Hacking

The word stealth has a secret meaning, where hacker can launch a virus or a worm with a backdoor and can thereby maintain a stealthy environment of operation and without the knowledge of the target. This stealth environment can stay in the system for a long time.

Stuxnet & Dugu

These two advance worms are reported to be written by organizations with advanced technical computing skills, and therefore are sponsored by nations, used to attack facilities in a cyber war with other nations for national security reasons. The Stuxnet worm used in destroying large numbers of center fusions of the Iranian nuclear plant. While Dugu is another version of the Stuxnet worm, and claimed to have been developed by the same group and nations, and the purpose to provide the greatest ability of spying and collecting information on individuals and companies. The use of Dugu is reported in Iran and other Middle Eastern countries.

Wireless (Wifi)

They can be both private wireless systems or networks (VPN) or public ones. Both of these systems provide any mobile and other PC based devices to connect to the router broadcasting the signals to network with the site or server containing the communication software system to wide world internet. Any mobile device either a phone, iPod, or portable computer can be connected with the installed Wifi application, and provide the ability to interconnect with the net.

References

1. ^ *"Building a Cyber Secure Plant".* Siemens. 30 September 2010. Retrieved 5 December 2010.
2. ^ *a b c* Robert McMillan (16 September 2010). *"Siemens: Stuxnet worm hit industrial systems".* Computerworld. Retrieved 16 September 2010.
3. ^ *"Last-minute paper: An in-depth look into Stuxnet".* Virus Bulletin.
4. ^ *"Stuxnet worm hits Iran nuclear plant staff computers".* BBC News. 26 September 2010.
5. ^ Nicolas Falliere (6 August 2010). *"Stuxnet Introduces the First Known Rootkits for Industrial Control Systems".* Symantec.
6. ^ *a b* *"Iran's Nuclear Agency Trying to Stop Computer Worm".* Tehran: Associated Press. 25 September 2010. Archived from the original on 25 September 2010. Retrieved 25 September 2010.
7. ^ *a b c d e* Gregg Keizer (16 September 2010). *"Is Stuxnet the 'best' malware ever?".* Infoworld. Retrieved 16 September 2010.
8. ^ *a b c d e f* Steven Cherry, with Ralph Langner (October 13, 2010). *"How Stuxnet Is Rewriting the Cyberterrorism Playbook".* IEEE Spectrum.
9. ^ *"Stuxnet Virus Targets and Spread Revealed".* BBC News. 15 February 2011. Retrieved 17 February 2011.
10. ^ *a b c d* Fildes, Jonathan (23 September 2010). *"Stuxnet worm 'targeted high-value Iranian assets'".* BBC News. Retrieved 23 September 2010.
11. ^ Beaumont, Claudine (23 September 2010). *"Stuxnet virus: worm 'could be aimed at high-profile Iranian*

targets'". London: The Daily Telegraph. Retrieved 28 September 2010.

12.   ^ *MacLean, William (24 September 2010). "UPDATE 2-Cyber attack appears to target Iran-tech firms". Reuters.*

13.   ^ *ComputerWorld (14 September 2010). "Siemens: Stuxnet worm hit industrial systems". Computerworld. Retrieved 3 October 2010.*

14.   ^ *"Iran Confirms Stuxnet Worm Halted Centrifuges". CBS News. 29 November 2010.*

15.   ^ a b *Ethan Bronner & William J. Broad: In a Computer Worm, a Possible Biblical Clue. In: NYTimes. 29 September 2010. Retrieved on 2 October 2010. (en)"Software smart bomb fired at Iranian nuclear plant: Experts". Economictimes.indiatimes.com. 24 September 2010. Retrieved 28 September 2010.*

16.   ^ *"Kaspersky Lab provides its insights on Stuxnet worm". Kaspersky (Russia). 24 September 2010.*

17.   ^ *"Stuxnet Questions and Answers - F-Secure Weblog". F-Secure (Finland). 1 October 2010.*

18.   ^ a b *Israel video shows Stuxnet as one of its successes*

19.   ^ *Markoff, John (11 February 2011). "Malware Aimed at Iran Hit Five Sites, Report Says". New York Times. p. 15.*

20.   ^ a b c d *Steven Cherry, with Larry Constantine (December 14, 2011). "Sons of Stuxnet". IEEE Spectrum.*

21.   ^ *Gary Samore speaking at the 10 December 2010 Washington Forum of the Foundation for Defense of Democracies in Washington DC, reported by C-Span and contained in the PBS program Need to Know ("Cracking the*

code: Defending against the superweapons of the 21st century cyberwar", 4 minutes into piece)

22. ^ *Krebs, Brian (17 July 2010). "Experts Warn of New Windows Shortcut Flaw". Krebs on Security. Retrieved 3 March 2011.*
23. ^ ªGross, *Michael Joseph (April 2011). "A Declaration of Cyber-War". Vanity Fair. Condé Nast.*
24. ^ ª"A *worm in the centrifuge: An unusually sophisticated cyber-weapon is mysterious but important". The Economist. 30 September 2010.*
25. ^ *Alexander Gostev (26 September 2010). "Myrtus and Guava: the epidemic, the trends, the numbers". Retrieved 22 January 2011.*
26. ^ ª b c *Aleksandr Matrosov, Eugene Rodionov, David Harley, and Juraj Malcho. "Stuxnet Under the Microscope" (PDF). Retrieved 24 September 2010.*
27. ^ *Sam Kiley. "Super Virus A Target For Cyber Terrorists". Retrieved 25 November 2010.*
28. ^ *Phil Muncaster. "Experts slam Stuxnet black market hype". Retrieved 6 November 2011.*
29. ^ *"W32.Stuxnet". Symantec. 17 September 2010. Retrieved 2 March 2011.*
30. ^ ª b c d e f g *Broad, William J.; Markoff, John; Sanger, David E. (15 January 2011). "Israel Tests on Worm Called Crucial in Iran Nuclear Delay". New York Times. Retrieved 16 January 2011.*
31. ^ *"Conficker Worm: Help Protect Windows from Conficker". Microsoft. 10 April 2009. Retrieved 6 December 2010.*
32. ^ ª b c d e f *Kim Zetter (23 September 2010). "Blockbuster Worm Aimed for Infrastructure, But No Proof Iran Nukes Were Target". Wired. Retrieved 24 September 2010.*

33.   ^ *Liam O Murchu (17 September 2010). "Stuxnet P2P component". Symantec. Retrieved 24 September 2010.*

34.   ^ a b c d e f g *"W32.Stuxnet Dossier". Symantec Corporation.*

35.   ^ *"Kaspersky Lab provides its insights on Stuxnet worm". Kaspersky Lab. 24 September 2010. Retrieved 27 September 2010.*

36.   ^ *Michael Joseph Gross (April 2011). "A Declaration of Cyber-War". Vanity Fair. Retrieved 4 March 2011.*

37.   ^ *Ralph Langner (14 September 2010). "Ralph's Step-By-Step Guide to Get a Crack at Stuxnet Traffic and Behaviour". Retrieved 4 March 2011.*

38.   ^ *Nicolas Falliere (26 September 2010). "Stuxnet Infection of Step 7 Projects". Symantec.*

39.   ^ *"Vulnerability Summary for CVE-2010-2772". National Vulnerability Database. 22 July 2010. Retrieved 7 December 2010.*

40.   ^ a b *Eric Chien (12 November 2010). "Stuxnet: A Breakthrough". Symantec. Retrieved 14 November 2010.*

41.   ^ a b *"SIMATIC WinCC / SIMATIC PCS 7: Information concerning Malware / Virus / Trojan". Siemens. Retrieved 24 September 2010.*

42.   ^ *Tom Espiner (20 July 2010). "Siemens warns Stuxnet targets of password risk". cnet. Retrieved 17 September 2010.*

43.   ^ *"Siemens: Stuxnet Worm Hit Industrial Systems". IDG News.*

44.   ^ *crve (17 September 2010). "Stuxnet also found at industrial plants in Germany". The H. Retrieved 18 September 2010.*

45.   ^ *"Repository of Industrial Security Incidents".* *Security Incidents Organization. Retrieved 14 October 2010.*

46.   ^ *"DHS National Cyber Security Division's CSSP".* *DHS. Retrieved 14 October 2010.*

47.   ^ *"ISA99, Industrial Automation and Control System Security". International Society of Automation. Retrieved 14 October 2010.*

48.   ^ *"Industrial communication networks – Network and system security – Part 2-1: Establishing an industrial automation and control system security program". International Electrotechnical Commission. Retrieved 14 October 2010.*

49.   ^ *"Chemical Sector Cyber Security Program". ACC ChemITC. Retrieved 14 October 2010.*

50.   ^ *"Pipeline SCADA Security Standard". API. Retrieved 19 November 2010.*

51.   ^ *Marty Edwards (Idaho National Laboratory) & Todd Stauffer (Siemens). "2008 Automation Summit: A User's Conference". United States Department of Homeland Security. p. 35.*

52.   ^ *"The Can of Worms Is Open-Now What?". ControlGlobal. Retrieved 14 October 2010.*

53.   ^ *a b c Halliday, Josh (24 September 2010). "Stuxnet worm is the 'work of a national government agency'". London: The Guardian. Retrieved 27 September 2010.*

54.   ^ *a b c Markoff, John (26 September 2010). "A Silent Attack, but Not a Subtle One". New York Times. Retrieved 27 September 2010.*

55.   ^ *Schneier, Bruce (6 October 2010). "The Story Behind The Stuxnet Virus". Forbes.*

56.   ^ *Bright, Arthur (1 October 2010). "Clues Emerge About Genesis of Stuxnet Worm". Christian Science Monitor. Retrieved 4 March 2011.*

57.   ^ *Langner, Ralph (February 2011). "Ralph Langner: Cracking Stuxnet, a 21st-century cyber weapon".*

58.   ^ *Robert McMillan (23 July 2010). "Iran was prime target of SCADA worm". Computerworld. Retrieved 17 September 2010.*

59.   ^ *Paul Woodward (22 September 2010). "Iran confirms Stuxnet found at Bushehr nuclear power plant". Warincontext.org. Retrieved 28 September 2010.*

60.   ^ *"6 mysteries about Stuxnet". Blog.foreignpolicy.com. Retrieved 28 September 2010.*

61.   ^ *Clayton, Mark (21 September 2010). "Stuxnet malware is 'weapon' out to destroy ... Iran's Bushehr nuclear plant?". Christian Science Monitor. Retrieved 23 September 2010.*

62.   ^ *Yossi Melman (28 September 2010). "'Computer virus in Iran actually targeted larger nuclear facility'". Retrieved 1 January 2011.*

63.   ^ *"Iranian Nuclear Program Plagued by Technical Difficulties". Globalsecuritynewswire.org. 23 November 2010. Retrieved 24 November 2010.*

64.   ^ *"Iran pauses uranium enrichment at Natanz nuclear plant". Haaretz.com. 24 November 2010. Retrieved 24 November 2010.*
      ^ *a b "The Stuxnet worm: A cyber-missile aimed at Iran?". The Economist. 24 September 2010. Retrieved 28 September 2010.*

65.   ^ *"Serious nuclear accident may lay behind Iranian nuke chief%27s mystery resignation". wikileaks. 16 July 2009. Retrieved 1 January 2011.*

66.   ^ *"IAEA Report on Iran". Institute for Science and International Security. 16 November 2010. Retrieved 1 January 2011.*

67.   ^ *a b c "Did Stuxnet Take Out 1,000 Centrifuges at the Natanz Enrichment Plant?". Institute for Science and International Security. 22 December 2010. Retrieved 27 December 2010.*

68.   ^ *"Stuxnet-Virus könnte tausend Uran-Zentrifugen zerstört haben". Der Spiegel. 26 December 2010. Retrieved 27 December 2010.*

69.   ^ *Stark, Holger (8 August 2011). "Mossad's Miracle Weapon: Stuxnet Virus Opens New Era of Cyber War". Der Spiegel.*

70.   ^ *Warrick, Joby, "Iran's Natanz nuclear facility recovered quickly from Stuxnet cyberattack", Washington Post, 16 February 2011, retrieved 17 February 2011.*

71.   ^ *"Signs of sabotage in Tehran's nuclear programme". Gulf News. 14 July 2010.*

72.   ^ *a b Dan Williams (7 July 2009). "Wary of naked force, Israel eyes cyberwar on Iran". Reuters.*

73.   ^ *Aneja, Atul (26 September 2010). "Under cyber-attack, says Iran". Chennai, India: The Hindu.*

74.   ^ *a b "Stuxnet worm rampaging through Iran: IT official". AFP. Archived from the original on 28 September 2010.*

75.   ^ *"IRAN: Speculation on Israeli involvement in malware computer attack". Los Angeles Times. 27 September 2010. Retrieved 28 September 2010.*

76.   ^ *a b Erdbrink, Thomas; Nakashima, Ellen (27 September 2010). "Iran struggling to contain 'foreign-made' 'Stuxnet' computer virus". Washington Post. Retrieved 28 September 2010.*

77.   ^ *"Ahmadinedschad räumt Virus-Attacke ein"*. *Der Spiegel*. 29 November 2010. Retrieved 29 December 2010.

78.   ^ *"Stuxnet: Ahmadinejad admits cyberweapon hit Iran nuclear program"*. *The Christian Science Monitor*. 30 November 2010. Retrieved 29 December 2010.

79.   ^ *a b*

http://www.wired.com/threatlevel/2010/11/stuxnet-sabotage-centrifuges/

80.   ^

http://www.foxnews.com/world/2012/01/11/report-bomb-kills-iran-university-professor/?test=latestnews

81.   ^ Monica Amarelo (21 January 2011). *"New FAS Report Demonstrates Iran Improved Enrichment in 2010"*. *Federation of American Scientists*.

82.   ^ *"Report: Iran's nuclear capacity unharmed, contrary to U.S. assessment"*. *Haaretz*. 22 January 2011.

83.   ^ Jeffrey Goldberg (22 January 2011). *"Report: Report: Iran's Nuclear Program Going Full Speed Ahead"*. *The Atlantic*.

84.   ^ Beaumont, Peter (30 September 2010). *"Stuxnet worm heralds new era of global cyberwar"*. London: Guardian.co.uk.

85.   ^ Hounshell, Blake (27 September 2010). *"6 mysteries about Stuxnet"*. *Foreign Policy*. Retrieved 28 September 2010.

86.   ^ *"Falkenrath Says Stuxnet Virus May Have Origin in Israel: Video. Bloomberg Television"*. 24 September 2010.

87.   ^ Dan Williams. *"Cyber takes centre stage in Israel's war strategy"*. *Reuters*, 28 September 2010.

88.   ^ Antonin Gregoire. *"Stuxnet, the real face of cyber warfare"*. *Iloubnan.info*, 25 November 2010.

89.   ^ *a b Broad, William J.; Sanger, David E. (18 November 2010). "Worm in Iran Can Wreck Nuclear Centrifuges". The New York Times.*

90.   ^ *Williams, Christoper (16 February 2011). "Israeli security chief celebrates Stuxnet cyber attack". The Telegraph (London). Retrieved 23 February 2011.*

91.   ^ *David Sanger (25 September 2010). "Iran Fights Malware Attacking Computers". New York Times. Retrieved 28 September 2010.*

92.   ^ *Iran/Critical National Infrastructure: Cyber Security Experts See The Hand Of Israel's Signals Intelligence Service In The "Stuxnet" Virus Which Has Infected Iranian Nuclear Facilities, 1 September 2010. [1].*

93.   ^ *Riddle, Warren (1 October 2010). "Mysterious 'Myrtus' Biblical Reference Spotted in Stuxnet Code". SWITCHED. Retrieved 6 October 2010.*

94.   ^ *"SCADA Systems Whitepaper". Motorola.*

95.   ^ *"Symantec Puts 'Stuxnet' Malware Under the Knife". PC Magazine.*

96.   ^ *"New Clues Point to Israel as Author of Blockbuster Worm, Or Not". Wired.*

97.   ^ *a b Reals, Tucker (24 September 2010). "Stuxnet Worm a U.S. Cyber-Attack on Iran Nukes?". CBS News.*

98.   ^ *Halliday, Josh (18 January 2011). "WikiLeaks: US advised to sabotage Iran nuclear sites by German thinktank". The Guardian (London). Retrieved 19 January 2011.*

99.   ^ *Kim Zetter (17 February 2011). "Cyberwar Issues Likely to Be Addressed Only After a Catastrophe". Wired. Retrieved 18 February 2011.*

100.   ^ *Chris Carroll (18 October 2011). "Cone of silence surrounds U.S. cyberwarfare". Stars and Stripes. Retrieved 30 October 2011.*

101.　　　　^ John Bumgarner (27 April 2010). "Computers as Weapons of War". IO Journal. Retrieved 30 October 2011.

102.　　　　^ "Iran blames U.S., Israel for Stuxnet malware" (SHTML). CBS News. April 16, 2011 10:10 AM. Retrieved 2012-1-15.

103.　　　　^ Carr, Jeffrey (14 December 2010). "Stuxnet's Finnish-Chinese Connection". Forbes. Retrieved 19 April 2011.

104.　　　　^ Clayton, Mark (24 September 2010). "Stuxnet worm mystery: What's the cyber weapon after?". Christian Science Monitor. Retrieved 21 January 2011.

105.　　　　^ Gaycken, Sandro (26 November 2010). "Stuxnet: Wer war's? Und wozu?". Die ZEIT. Retrieved 19 April 2011.

106.　　　　^ Hopkins, Nick (31 May 2011). "UK developing cyber-weapons programme to counter cyber war threat" (in English). The Guardian (United Kingdom). Retrieved 31 May 2011.

107.　　　　^ "Duqu: A Stuxnet-like malware found in the wild, technical report". Laboratory of Cryptography of Systems Security (CrySyS). 14 October 2011.

108.　　　　^ "Statement on Duqu's initial analysis". Laboratory of Cryptography of Systems Security (CrySyS). 21 October 2011. Retrieved 25 October 2011.

109.　　　　^ "W32.Duqu – The precursor to the next Stuxnet (Version 1.2)". Symantec. 20 October 2011. Retrieved 25 October 2011.

110.　　　　^ Jim Finkle (28 December 2011). "Stuxnet weapon has at least 4 cousins: researchers". Reuters.

Further reading

- Langner, Ralph (March 2011). "Ralph Langner: Cracking Stuxnet, a 21st-century cyber weapon". TED. TED Conferences, LLC. Retrieved 13 May 2011.
- "The short path from cyber missiles to dirty digital bombs". Blog. Langner Communications GmbH. 26 December 2010. Retrieved 13 May 2011.
- Falliere, Nicolas (21 September 2010). "Exploring Stuxnet's PLC Infection Process". Blogs: Security Response. Symantec. Retrieved 13 May 2011.
- "Stuxnet Questions and Answers". News from the Lab. F-Secure. 1 October 2010. Retrieved 13 May 2011.
- Mills, Elinor (5 October 2010). "Stuxnet: Fact vs. theory". CNET News (CBS Interactive). Retrieved 13 May 2011.
- Dang, Bruce; Ferrie, Peter (28 December 2010). "27C3: Adventures in analyzing Stuxnet". CCC-TV. Chaos Computer Club e.V.. Retrieved 13 May 2011.
- Oracle & SAP websites on security issues and software systems offers to public and private entities.
- Russinovich, Mark (30 March 2011). "Analyzing a Stuxnet Infection with the Sysinternals Tools, Part 1". Mark's Blog. MSDN Blogs (Microsoft Corporation). Retrieved 13 May 2011.
- Zetter, Kim (11 July 2011). "How Digital Detectives Deciphered Stuxnet, the Most Menacing Malware in History".
- Cyber War: The Next Threat to National Security what to do about it, by Richard Clarke, April 10, 2012

Index

A

agenda, 3, 5, 13, 32, 36, 44, 72, 74, 85, 88, 94, 142, 176, 179, 181, 205, 213, 222, 225, 260, 283

anti viruses, 187, 209

anti-viruses, 93, 95, 96, 118, 142, 211, 254

Aramco, 27, 187, 201, 211, 254, 282

ATM, 73, 119, 199, 238

Attacks, 10, 42

B

backbone Tier 1 type, 287

banking, 3, 21, 65, 90, 106, 176, 198, 212, 217

Banking Supervisory Rules,, 198

Bills of Materials, 157

black market, 6, 27, 32, 38, 43, 58, 70, 71, 73, 251

blackout, 202, 223, 224

bureaucratic, 5, 285

C

central cyber command for Qatar (CCC), 229

centralized military grade cyber center, 221

centrifuges, 16, 17, 20

CERT, 11, 195, 199, 219, 220, 252, 253, 256, 258, 259, 261, 272, 281

China, 3, 6, 7, 8, 13, 36, 37, 49, 53, 55, 58, 67, 78, 127, 188, 204, 210, 226, 234, 237, 238, 239, 240, 245, 246, 247, 248, 249, 276, 284

communications networks, 4

consumer-centric, 165

critical infrastructures, 231, 279

Cyber, 10, 11, 13, 23, 24, 31, 37, 42, 78, 104, 123, 124, 127, 148, 161, 168, 169, 176, 180, 189, 190, 191, 192, 193, 196, 197, 198, 200, 204, 206, 209, 214, 216, 222, 225, 229, 247, 250, 251, 252, 253, 257, 258, 262, 263, 264, 268, 271, 277, 281, 284, 287

cyber command and control centers, 221

cyber espionage, 38, 52, 56, 79

cyber regulatory, 204

cyber security road map, 118

cyber security strategy, 107, 109, 115, 180, 277

cyber technology, 18, 58, 193, 209, 276, 287, 288

cyber wars, 10, 13, 35, 56, 205, 252

D

Database Security, 159, 162

DDoS, 21, 22, 25, 32, 293, 294

developing nations, 4, 12, 57, 78, 128, 153, 177, 204, 215

Digital Cluster, 193

dissertation, 6

DoD, 148, 151, 158

Dugu, 25, 26, 79, 297

E

Eastern European, 77

education, 3, 31, 110, 118, 159, 165, 178, 261, 264, 266

e-government, 5, 233, 282

encryption, 12, 29, 84, 85, 90, 130, 148, 150, 154, 160, 161, 268 enrichment, 14, 16, 19, 24

ERP, 145, 146

Estonia, 21, 25, 55

F

FBI, 31, 43, 48, 51, 52, 58

Federal Bureau of Investigation, 43

FireEye, 31, 82, 83

firewalls, 5, 61, 62, 88, 92, 93, 94, 111,
115, 117, 186, 192, 199, 210, 214,
220, 231, 245, 250, 258, 259, 279, 287

Flame, 25, 27, 29, 79, 96

G

GCC headquarters, 171, 285

GCC-Gateway, 5

Georgia, 21, 23, 25, 55

Gulf, 1, 11, 176

H

hacking penetration testing, 112

hacktivists, 3, 7, 68

Huawei, 8

I

IBM, 8, 146, 164, 171, 238, 278, 295

Identity & Access Management, 158

IMF, 42, 43, 44, 184

implementation, 1, 137, 154, 191

installation, 173

insurances, 116, 120

International Monetary Fund, 42

intranet, 35, 55, 217, 243, 248

intrusion-detection, 5, 27, 46, 88, 92, 93,
94, 111, 117, 185, 186, 192, 209, 210,
220, 231, 245, 250, 254, 256, 258, 259

Iranian, 14, 15, 19, 21, 24, 79, 130, 139,
203, 206, 297

K

Kenyan, 125, 126, 128

Kuwait, 168, 202, 223, 224, 283

L

law enforcement agencies, 131, 132, 134,
226

Linux operating system, 8

logic bombs, 3, 13, 35, 37, 123, 222

M

Macintosh operating system, 7

mainframe, 43, 217

McAfee, 207

Microsoft Windows, 7, 65, 94, 106, 148,
236, 239

Middle East, 25, 26, 32, 38, 133, 137, 166,
197, 209, 232, 247, 250

military, 6, 10, 24, 27, 37, 53, 68, 79, 123,
127, 128, 137, 145, 151, 164, 171,
174, 206, 211, 213, 214, 215, 216,
217, 221, 225, 227, 230, 231, 232,
234, 252, 256, 257, 260, 262, 264,
265, 266, 268, 270, 273, 277, 279,
281, 284, 285, 286, 287, 288

mission- critical, 99

mobility, 64, 71, 115, 130, 134, 136, 137,
141, 152, 153, 154, 156, 164, 166,
169, 218, 233

model, 7, 8, 231, 234, 240, 248, 250, 255,
256, 265

multinationals, 111

N

national security, 11, 85, 125, 178, 181,
194, 197, 201, 206, 215, 217, 221,
225, 237, 247, 250, 259, 271, 277,
281, 285, 286, 297

Nato, 6, 11, 85, 281, 285, 286, 287, 288

NSA, 51, 270

Nuclear, 14, 206

O

Obama, 51, 52, 85, 257

oil and gas, 1, 3, 28, 31, 82, 117, 169, 176, 187, 193, 208, 212, 233, 250, 258, 276, 282

Olympics, 180

P

penetration testing, 111, 113

PLC, 17

power grid systems, 258

Prime Minister office (PMO), 255

Programming Logic Controller, 17

Q

Qatar, 1, 2, 28, 39, 75, 117, 118, 120, 122, 129, 147, 153, 155, 164, 168, 169, 170, 179, 180, 183, 187, 190, 192, 193, 196, 197, 198, 200, 209, 210, 213, 214, 215, 216, 217, 220, 221, 222, 226, 230, 231, 232, 233, 234, 240, 248, 250, 251, 253, 254, 255, 257, 258, 259, 260, 261, 264, 265, 269, 271, 273, 274, 278, 279, 281, 282, 286, 289

R

Ras Gas, 197, 200, 211

Rasgas, 27, 254, 282

reconnaissance, 136, 291

redundant, 97, 99, 214, 218

response emergency, 4, 212

road map, 7, 214, 232, 251, 252, 262, 273, 279

S

satellite, 10, 20, 98, 132, 172

Saudi Stock Exchange, 32

SCADA, 16, 34, 218

SEA, 38, 40

Siemens's, 16

signature certification, 18

simulation, 111, 113

skimmers, 60, 68, 73

Snowden, 84, 134, 237

Spear Phishing, 44

spy, 10, 12, 20, 26, 72, 76, 79, 85, 86, 130, 134, 142, 150, 161, 188, 226, 269

stealth, 18, 26, 68, 69, 71, 80, 87, 95, 113, 140, 142, 205, 211, 294, 296

Stuxnet, 14, 15, 17, 18, 19, 25, 27, 29, 79, 96, 139, 205, 297

Supervisory Control and Data Acquisition, 17, 34

Symantec, 207, 299, 301, 305, 306

Syrian, 24, 38, 39, 40

Syrian Electronic Army, 38, 39

T

Taiwan, 19, 27

Tallinn, 23, 24

techno-criminals, 68, 73

terrorists, 70, 225, 227

training, 24, 62, 69, 78, 92, 128, 165, 166, 179, 181, 193, 216, 253, 260, 261, 263, 264, 266, 271, 276, 287

trapdoors, 3, 13, 37, 123

V

viruses, 3, 5, 13, 16, 27, 32, 46, 48, 50, 52, 67, 69, 78, 79, 80, 81, 85, 88, 89, 93, 94, 95, 97, 98, 100, 107, 111, 115, 116, 117, 123, 124, 137, 139, 140, 148, 153, 156, 171, 181, 184, 185, 186, 192, 195, 199, 205, 207, 208, 209, 210, 214, 220, 222, 231, 237, 240, 244, 245, 250, 251, 253, 256, 258, 259, 261, 279, 282, 283, 287, 288, 290, 292, 294

visions, 2, 215, 233

VoIP, 133, 134, 135, 175

W

Websites hackers, 226

WickiLeak, 151

wifi, 71, 141

Windows operating system, 7, 16, 19, 26, 29, 81

World Bank, 43

World Cup, 2, 193, 222, 233, 250

World War II, 84

worms, 3, 6, 13, 20, 21, 24, 48, 50, 52, 67, 69, 78, 79, 80, 81, 93, 94, 95, 96, 98, 100, 113, 115, 116, 118, 123, 124, 128, 139, 140, 171, 181, 184, 186, 195, 205, 207, 209, 211, 222, 237, 251, 261, 282, 283, 287, 288, 290, 292, 294, 295, 297

Z

Zero-day exploit, 16

www.ingramcontent.com/pod-product-compliance
Lightning Source LLC
Chambersburg PA
CBHW070938050326
40689CB00014B/3255